Suicidal Behavior

About the Author

Richard T. McKeon, PhD, MPH, received his doctorate in clinical psychology from the University of Arizona, and a master of public health degree in Health Administration from Columbia University. He has spent most of his career working in community mental health, including 11 years as director of a psychiatric emergency service and 4 years as associate administrator/clinical director of a hospital-based community mental health center in Newton, New Jersey. He established the first evidence-based treatment program for chronically suicidal borderline patients in the state of New Jersey utilizing Marsha Linehan's Dialectical Behavior Therapy. In 2001, he was awarded an American Psychological Association Congressional Fellowship and worked for US Senator Paul Wellstone, covering health and mental health policy issues. He spent 5 years on the Board of the American Association of Suicidology as Clinical Division Director and has also served on the Board of the Division of Clinical Psychology of the American Psychological Association. He is currently Chief of the Suicide Prevention Branch for the Substance Abuse and Mental Health Services Administration in the US Department of Health and Human Services. In 2009, he was appointed by the Secretary of Defense to the Department of Defense Task Force on Suicide Prevention in the Military. He also serves as Co-Chair of the Federal Working Group on Suicide Prevention and participated in the development of the World Suicide Report for the World Health Organization

Advances in Psychotherapy – Evidence-Based Practice

Series Editor
Danny Wedding, PhD, MPH, Saybrook University, Oakland, CA

Associate Editors
Jonathan S. Comer, PhD, Professor of Psychology and Psychiatry, Director of Mental Health Interventions and Technology (MINT) Program, Center for Children and Families, Florida International University, Miami, FL
J. Kim Penberthy, PhD, ABPP, Professor of Psychiatry & Neurobehavioral Sciences, University of Virginia, Charlottesville, VA
Kenneth E. Freedland, PhD, Professor of Psychiatry and Psychology, Washington University School of Medicine, St. Louis, MO
Linda C. Sobell, PhD, ABPP, Professor, Center for Psychological Studies, Nova Southeastern University, Ft. Lauderdale, FL

The basic objective of this series is to provide therapists with practical, evidence-based treatment guidance for the most common disorders seen in clinical practice – and to do so in a reader-friendly manner. Each book in the series is both a compact "how-to" reference on a particular disorder for use by professional clinicians in their daily work and an ideal educational resource for students as well as for practice-oriented continuing education.

The most important feature of the books is that they are practical and easy to use: All are structured similarly and all provide a compact and easy-to-follow guide to all aspects that are relevant in real-life practice. Tables, boxed clinical "pearls," marginal notes, and summary boxes assist orientation, while checklists provide tools for use in daily practice.

Continuing Education Credits

Psychologists and other healthcare providers may earn five continuing education credits for reading the books in the *Advances in Psychotherapy* series and taking a multiple-choice exam. This continuing education program is a partnership of Hogrefe Publishing and the National Register of Health Service Psychologists. Details are available at https://www.hogrefe.com/us/cenatreg

The National Register of Health Service Psychologists is approved by the American Psychological Association to sponsor continuing education for psychologists. The National Register maintains responsibility for this program and its content.

Advances in Psychotherapy – Evidence-Based Practice, Volume 14

Suicidal Behavior

2nd edition

Richard T. McKeon
Former Clinical Division Director, American Association of Suicidology

Library of Congress of Congress Cataloging in Publication information for the print version of this book is available via the Library of Congress Marc Database under the Library of Congress Control Number 2021944412

Library and Archives Canada Cataloguing in Publication

Title: Suicidal behavior / Richard T. McKeon, former Clinical Division Director, American Association of Suicidology.
Names: McKeon, Richard T., author.
Series: Advances in psychotherapy--evidence-based practice ; v. 14.
Description: 2nd edition. | Series statement: Advances in psychotherapy--evidence-based practice ; volume 14 | Includes bibliographical references.
Identifiers: Canadiana (print) 20210314818 | Canadiana (ebook) 20210314974 | ISBN 9780889375062 (softcover) | ISBN 9781616765064 (PDF) | ISBN 9781613345061 (EPUB)
Subjects: LCSH: Suicidal behavior—Prevention. | LCSH: Suicidal behavior—Treatment.
Classification: LCC RC569 .M41 2021 | DDC 616.85/8445—dc23

© 2022 by Hogrefe Publishing

www.hogrefe.com

The authors and publisher have made every effort to ensure that the information contained in this text is in accord with the current state of scientific knowledge, recommendations, and practice at the time of publication. In spite of this diligence, errors cannot be completely excluded. Also, due to changing regulations and continuing research, information may become outdated at any point. The authors and publisher disclaim any responsibility for any consequences which may follow from the use of information presented in this book.

Registered trademarks are not noted specifically as such in this publication. The use of descriptive names, registered names, and trademarks does not imply, even in the absence of a specific statement, that such names are exempt from the relevant protective laws and regulations and therefore free for general use.

The cover image is an agency photo depicting models. Use of the photo on this publication does not imply any connection between the content of this publication and any person depicted in the cover image.
Cover image: © borchee – iStock.com

PUBLISHING OFFICES

USA:	Hogrefe Publishing Corporation, 44 Merrimac St., Suite 207, Newburyport, MA 01950 Phone 978 255 3700; E-mail customerservice@hogrefe.com
EUROPE:	Hogrefe Publishing GmbH, Merkelstr. 3, 37085 Göttingen, Germany Phone +49 551 99950 0, Fax +49 551 99950 111; E-mail publishing@hogrefe.com

SALES & DISTRIBUTION

USA:	Hogrefe Publishing, Customer Services Department, 30 Amberwood Parkway, Ashland, OH 44805 Phone 800 228 3749, Fax 419 281 6883; E-mail customerservice@hogrefe.com
UK:	Hogrefe Publishing, c/o Marston Book Services Ltd., 160 Eastern Ave., Milton Park, Abingdon, OX14 4SB Phone +44 1235 465577, Fax +44 1235 465556; E-mail direct.orders@marston.co.uk
EUROPE:	Hogrefe Publishing, Merkelstr. 3, 37085 Göttingen, Germany Phone +49 551 99950 0, Fax +49 551 99950 111; E-mail publishing@hogrefe.com

OTHER OFFICES

CANADA:	Hogrefe Publishing Corporation, 82 Laird Drive, East York, Ontario M4G 3V1
SWITZERLAND:	Hogrefe Publishing, Länggass-Strasse 76, 3012 Bern

No part of this book may be reproduced, stored in a retrieval system or transmitted, in any form or by any means, electronic, mechanical, photocopying, microfilming, recording or otherwise, without written permission from the publisher.

Printed and bound in the USA

ISBN 978-0-88937-506-2 (print) • ISBN 978-1-61676-506-4 (PDF) • ISBN 978-1-61334-506-1 (EPUB)
https://doi.org/10.1027/00506-000

Acknowledgments

I would like to acknowledge all those who have made this book possible, including the publisher, Hogrefe Publishing, and all the staff who contributed to this effort. I would especially like to thank series editor Danny Wedding for supporting the 2nd edition of this book on suicidal behavior in the series *Advances in Psychotherapy – Evidence-Based Practice.* His guidance and assistance during the development of this manuscript was invaluable. I would also like to thank Robert Dimbleby at Hogrefe Publishing for his support and encouragement over the years.

It is of particular importance for me to express my gratitude to all those who have shared their stories, their pain, and their hopes with me over the years, including all those I have worked with in community mental health and all those who have shared their stories with me across the country. All that I know I learned from them. To all the colleagues I have worked with to prevent suicide, whether we have worked together in emergency rooms or on conference calls, in therapy groups or in symposiums, thank you for sustaining me in our shared vision of reducing the tragic loss of lives to suicide. I must also acknowledge all those I have met who have survived the loss of a loved one to suicide, but who have utilized their grief to insist we must do better, and in so doing have transformed the priorities of a nation.

Finally, this book would not have been possible without the support of my family. I would like to thank my wife, Liz, for her advice, love, editing, and encouragement, my daughters Britt and Shauna, my niece Katie and nephew Michael, and my grandchildren Samantha and Teddy, who are my sources of hope for the future.

Disclaimer

All opinions expressed in this book are those of the author alone and do not represent the views of the Substance Abuse and Mental Health Services Administration.

Dedication

This book is dedicated to the memory of my sister Kathy, who taught me how important it is to fight for every hour of life.

Contents

1

Description

Suicide is a tragic end to an individual's life, a devastating loss to families and friends, a diminishment of our communities, and a public health crisis around the world. For clinicians, losing a patient to suicide is probably our worst fear. In 2018, over 48,000 Americans died by suicide (CDC, 2021) and suicide rates have increased in 49 of the 50 states (Stone et al., 2018). Worldwide, it is estimated 800,000 people die by suicide each year, more than are lost to homicide or to war (WHO, 2019b), leading the World Health Organization to issue the first world suicide report, *Preventing Suicide: A Global Imperative* (WHO, 2014), urging nations around the globe to adopt national suicide prevention strategies and programs. In addition, self-inflicted injury is estimated to account for 1.4% of the total burden of disease worldwide (World Federation for Mental Health, 2006). Yet, despite the magnitude of these losses, or perhaps because of the depth of our distress and uncertainty when confronted with acts of deliberate self-destruction, we have tended as a society to look away and not grapple with the issue of suicidal behavior, despite the tragic toll it exacts.

Worldwide, about 800,000 people die by suicide each year, more than are lost to homicide or to war

Kay Redfield Jamison has eloquently stated that in dealing with suicide, "The gap between what we know and what we do is lethal" (Jamison, 1999). In the two decades since Dr. Jamison wrote these words, we have learned much more, yet the lethal gap continues. In *Night Falls Fast,* her first-person account of her struggles with intense suicidal urges, she emphasizes the powerful link between mental illness and suicide, and the disturbing reality that the majority of those who die by suicide have never received mental health treatment (Jamison, 1999). Despite the fact that we know how to treat successfully many of the conditions that are risk factors for suicide, such as depression, substance abuse, and bipolar illness, so many of those who die by suicide never receive such treatment for these disorders (Luoma et al., 2002). When they do receive treatment, often this treatment does not focus on their suicidality, despite clear evidence that such a focus reduces suicidal behavior.

"The gap between what we know and what we do is lethal" (Kay Redfield Jamison)

While the gap between what we know and what we do is undoubtedly lethal, there is still much more that we need to know. For, example, we do not have controlled trial research that confirms that inpatient treatment is effective in preventing suicide, let alone under what circumstances hospitalization might be effective. We lack this knowledge even though reliance on inpatient hospitalization is a cornerstone of how almost all mental health systems respond to suicidal individuals. The face of inpatient psychiatric care in the US has drastically changed overtime and in a Cochrane systematic review published in 2014 high income countries around the world the lengths of stay for people with serious mental illness were found to have been reduced drastically

(Babalola et al., 2014) This has amounted to a major, uncontrolled experiment in how we treat suicidal people, yet we know little about the impact such massive changes have had. In addition, despite the fact that involuntary hospitalization laws across the United States utilize the concept of imminent risk, the research on acute risk factors for suicide measures risk in months, not in hours or days (Simon, 2006). While the emerging literature on predictive analytics for suicide is encouraging, it also speaks to suicide risk in months (Kessler et al., 2015). Predictive analytics may be most helpful by identifying those who are at significantly lower risk of suicide, and those who may become suicidal months in the future, rather than identifying those who will die by suicide in the coming hours or days. Simon (2006) has characterized imminent risk prediction as an illusion. Because of this, Hogan (personal communication, February 2020) has argued that we should stop chasing the illusion of individual prediction and focus instead on improving care for groups identified as at elevated risk. Just as cardiology focuses less on predicting when an individual will die from a heart attack, and more on focusing on reducing risk in high-risk groups, so too should mental health focus on improving care and intervention using the accumulating evidence we now have for groups who have been identified as being at elevated risk.

We need to focus on improving care for groups at elevated risk

We also need to know much more about how to successfully engage at risk people in treatment. The Utah Youth Suicide study showed that even though 44% of youth who died by suicide and had received psychiatric diagnoses had been prescribed psychotropic medication, upon autopsy none

of the youth were found to have either therapeutic or sub-therapeutic medication levels (Moskos et al., 2005), In the United States, the National Violent Death Reporting System has shown that while approximately half of women who die by suicide are receiving some type of mental health treatment, more than 70% of men are not (Niederkrotenthaler et al., 2014). Given the preponderance of suicides among males in the United States as well as in many other countries (Kapur & Goldney, 2019), this leads to the need to better understand what drives help seeking among men, particularly for mental healthcare and particularly when the depth of pain leads to suicidal thoughts or behaviors. This likely involves both men's interpretation of their own experience of suicidality as well as their views about the kind of help is available and its potential for alleviating their pain. How people at risk for suicide respond not only to the interventions we have but the way they can be accessed, and how we can promote collaborations to stay safe are also critical issues.

The field of suicide prevention has begun to advance the state of knowledge by examining the full range of suicidal behavior as an outcome variable, rather than focusing exclusively on deaths by suicide. Demonstrating reductions in deaths by suicide in controlled trials is very challenging because the number of participants in the study needs to be extremely large. For example, a WHO study that demonstrated reduction in death by suicide by an emergency room intervention and follow-up with those who had attempted suicide had 1,867 participants from five different countries (Fleischmann et al., 2008). Because suicidal ideation and attempts are much more common than death by suicide, research demonstrating the effectiveness of interventions are much more feasible. Both treatment and prevention studies have demonstrated reductions in suicide attempts (Allmon et al., 1991; Aseltine &

DeMartino, 2004; Brown et al., 2005; May et al., 2005). While some would argue that those who die by suicide are a very different population from those who attempt suicide, and that therefore findings based on research on suicide attempters cannot be generalized to those who die by suicide, research that highlights both the subsequent mortality and morbidity associated with suicide attempts (Beautrais, 2004) supports the importance of research focused on this population. Further, even though suicidal ideation by itself is not considered to be a strong predictor of death by suicide given that the overwhelming majority of people who think about killing themselves do not go on to die by suicide, suicidal ideation is invariably associated with intense pain and despair and such suffering deserves effective treatment in its own right. Suicidal ideation, suicide attempts, and death by suicide are closely linked clinical phenomenon even if they are found in overlapping and not identical populations. Only by considering suicidal ideation, suicide attempts and death by suicide together do we see the true scope and impact of suicidality nationally and worldwide.

Both treatment and prevention studies have demonstrated reductions in suicidal behavior

Advances in violence research focusing on imminent and near-term risk have taken place in part because of a willingness to look at violent behavior as a continuum, rather than focusing solely on homicide. As a result, findings with significant clinical implications, such as the ability to assess the risk of violent behavior on inpatient units at the time of hospital admission (McNiel et al., 2003), have occurred in violence research. Such findings in the violence risk literature suggest that while evidence identifying imminent risk for suicidal behavior may now be lacking, it may be possible to obtain this evidence, particularly if we include all suicidal behavior and not only fatal suicidal behavior.

Additional research has demonstrated reductions in suicidal thinking or in suicidal intent (Bruce et al., 2004; Gould et al., 2007). While reducing suicidal ideation or intent certainly does not assure a concomitant reduction in suicide attempts or in death by suicide, such cognitive phenomena are clearly very meaningful intermediate variables as they are very likely preconditions for suicide attempts or death by suicide.

The failure in the past, both nationally and internationally, to focus on suicide prevention has thankfully been changing. In a study of nations implementing national suicide prevention strategies, Lewitzka and colleagues (2019) showed a statistically significant decline in suicide in Norway, Sweden, Finland, and Australia compared to control countries. The decline was strongest in males, particularly ages 25–44 years and 45–64 years.

In 2001, the US Department of Health and Human Services, on behalf of a coalition of federal agencies and private nonprofit organizations, issued the *National Strategy for Suicide Prevention (NSSP)*. In 2012, to capitalize on advances in suicide prevention over the past decade, a revised *National Strategy for Suicide Prevention* was released by the Office of the Surgeon General and the National Action Alliance for Suicide Prevention (US Department of Health and Human Services, 2012). WHO released its first suicide report, *Preventing Suicide: A Global Imperative*, in 2014, which called on nations to develop national programs or strategies for suicide prevention and highlighted efforts in nations as diverse as Japan, Scotland and Chile (WHO, 2014b). The Substance Abuse and Mental Health Services Administration

(SAMHSA) has released a report assessing implementation of the US national strategy (2018) and WHO has released a report assessing international efforts to implement national programs and strategies (WHO, 2018).

The revised US *National Strategy for Suicide Prevention* contains 13 goals and 60 objectives as part of a comprehensive public health strategy to reduce suicide and suicide attempts (US Department of Health and Human Services, 2012). The US national strategy has been adopted as a model for the majority of states which have developed state suicide prevention plans as well as a model for efforts focusing on specific high-risk groups such as the *National Strategy for Preventing Veteran Suicide* (US Department of Veterans Affairs, 2018) and the *Department of Defense Strategy for Suicide Prevention* (US Department of Defense, 2015). The national strategy also contains numerous objectives that challenge the mental health field to improve its readiness and capacity to prevent suicides. Implementation of these objectives holds promise for improving the treatment and management of suicidal people. The national strategy calls for the systematic implementation in clinical settings of all that we now know in clinical suicidology. One significant development called for by the US national strategy has been the incorporation of these advances as a clinical bundle or set of protocols under the rubric of the aspirational goal of zero suicide among the people under our care. The call in the US national strategy for zero suicide as a goal reflects the belief that aiming for zero is much more likely to lead to the kind of transformational change that is needed in healthcare systems to overcome the frequently pervasive sense of fatalism about preventing suicide. The possibility of making significant reductions in the rate of suicide among patients receiving mental healthcare has already been demonstrated in England which lowered the rate of suicide by more than 50% despite an increase in the number of mental health patients (Appleby et al., 2019). This was accomplished by systematically implementing recommendations from a series of annual reports called the *National Confidential Inquiry Into Suicide and Homicide*. The efforts in England to reduce suicide among those receiving mental healthcare are perhaps the most impressive of any nation in the world.

In England, there has been a 50% reduction in the suicide rate for mental health patients

Additionally, the US national strategy objectives include the routine incorporation of training in suicide risk assessment, management, and treatment into graduate training programs and into continuing education programs. Bongar (2002) reviewed how frequently formal training in the study of suicide or the assessment or treatment of suicidal patients was offered in graduate school training in the mental health professions and found that the frequency of such training ranged from 29% to 41% in studies of psychology, social work, and marriage and family therapy training programs.

Many mental health professionals receive little or no training in suicide prevention

It is clear that many mental health professionals receive little or no formal training in suicide prevention. Yet, most Americans probably assume that when they go to see a mental health professional, they are seeing someone who has been trained to assess, manage, and treat suicide risk and behavior. The importance of continuing education has been demonstrated in England where training in suicide prevention every 3 years was shown to be one of the key variables associated with lowering rates of suicide among those receiving mental healthcare (While et al., 2012). In the United States, a growing number of states have recognized the critical importance of health and mental health professionals being trained in suicide prevention and have instituted requirements for licensure or for continuing education. The state of Washington was the first such state and now requires all health professionals to be trained. California now also requires psychologists and other mental health professionals to demonstrate such training as a requirement for licensure, and New Hampshire, Kentucky, and other states have instituted similar requirements (American Foundation for Suicide Prevention, 2016).

Clinical training in suicide prevention was associated with decreases in suicide in England

Other crucial national strategy objectives emphasize the importance of developing guidelines for assessing and managing risk in mental health systems, for improving continuity of care of suicidal patients following discharge from emergency departments (EDs) and inpatient psychiatric units, and for more effectively involving and educating families of patients who are at risk of suicide.

While students in graduate training in the mental health professions may all too often receive little training in suicide risk assessment, treatment, or management, this does not mean that students are not treating patients at significant risk. In fact, one study found that one in nine graduate students in psychology had experienced a patient's suicide at some point during their training, 40% of them prior to their internship (Kleespies et al. 1993). Findings such as these underscore the importance of training for graduate students in suicide prevention, not only to be a competent mental health professional, but also for trainees to be adequately prepared to treat those suicidal patients they will encounter during their training.

Treating suicidal patients requires numerous skills and competencies, including skills in assessment, treatment planning, managing crises, and knowledge of applicable laws and regulations. All these must occur within the context of clinicians having a clear understanding of their own feelings, attitudes, and judgments regarding suicidal behavior. We all react strongly to witnessing self-destruction and experience fear and anxiety about potentially losing someone we care about to suicide. These reactions are based on our own past personal and professional experiences, including our own or our family or friends' experience of suicidal behavior. Understanding these reactions is essential to competently treating suicidal individuals.

I first experienced the loss of a patient to suicide when I was a psychology intern. I was providing outpatient psychotherapy to a patient that our entire treatment team believed to be at high, continuing risk for suicide. The reason for this perception of elevated risk was solidly grounded in what we now know about heightened suicide risk. He had a past history of suicide attempts, and these attempts were high in lethality, including one attempt during which he cut his own throat. A past history of suicide attempts, particularly attempts that are high in potential lethality, is the single, strongest predictor of ultimate death by suicide (Hawton, 2005). This was a man who had clearly demonstrated that he had the capacity for lethal self-destruction. Because of an increase in his level of depression, hopelessness, and suicidal ideation, he was hospitalized on an inpatient psychiatric unit. While he was hospitalized, I needed to return to my university to defend my doctoral dissertation. Upon my return to my internship, I learned that he had been discharged from the inpatient unit to a day hospital but had taken a fatal overdose within 48 hours of his discharge. This powerful personal experience made me appreciate something I would later learn from the literature: The period immediately after an inpatient discharge, indeed after any episode of acute care for suicidality, contains significant, but frequently unrecognized risk for suicide.

In this book, I use the phrase "died by suicide" rather than the more common term "committed suicide." I use this term out of respect to the countless family members who have lost a loved one to suicide. They have pointed out that we frequently use the word "commit" in contexts such as "commit a crime" or "commit a sin," and that suicide, though in the past treated as both a crime and a sin, is neither.

1.1 Terminology

Suicidal thoughts or behavior are not limited to any single diagnostic group or condition. Death by suicide occurs with distressing frequency among many different illnesses, including mood disorders, substance abuse disorders, schizophrenia, and personality disorders. In 2002 the Institute of Medicine (IOM) summarized the state of research in suicide and suicide prevention and reported that in the US over 90% of suicides are associated with mental illness or substance abuse disorders (Institute of Medicine et al., 2002). While the recent CDC Vital Signs study (Stone et al., 2018) estimated that only about 50% of suicides were associated with a known mental health condition, this did not take into account substance abuse problems as well as mental health conditions that may have been undiagnosed.

Suicidal behavior is not a DSM-5 diagnosis, although suicidal behavior disorder is proposed as a disorder for further study. This diagnosis would be given to individuals who made a suicide attempt within the past 2 years. Additionally, suicide crisis syndrome (Shuck et al., 2019) and acute suicidal affective disturbance (Joiner et al., 2018) have both been proposed for consideration as new diagnoses based on the observation that a rapidly emerging acute suicidal state frequently occurs before a suicide attempt. Currently, two DSM-5 diagnoses reference suicidality (see Box 1). Of note, the DSM-5 also introduces the category of nonsuicidal self-injury where the absence of suicidal intent is a defining characteristic. However, the relationship between nonsuicidal self-injury and suicidal behavior is complex and nuanced (Klonsky et al., 2013). The 10th revision of the *International Classification of Diseases* (ICD-10-CM; WHO, 2019a) includes codes for classifying external causes of injury (E-codes). These codes are an important mechanism for surveillance of suicide attempts, particularly in hospital settings, and are used to distinguish between intentional and nonintentional injuries. The ICD also provides codes for overdose and poisoning in an appendix labeled overdose. These are used to code this frequent method for suicide attempts, as well as to code for accidental overdoses.

Box 1
DSM-5 Diagnoses Referencing Suicidal Behavior (APA, 2013)

Diagnostic criteria for 296.xx major depressive episode

Criteria 9 – recurrent thoughts of suicide (not just fear of dying), recurrent suicidal ideation without specific plan, or a suicide attempt or a specific plan for committing suicide

Diagnostic criteria for 301.83 borderline personality disorder

Criteria 5 – recurrent suicidal behavior, gestures, threats, or self-mutilating behavior

Suicide behavior disorder (under study)

- suicide attempt initiated within the past 2 years
- does not include nonsuicidal self-injury
- does not include suicidal ideation without an attempt

Nonsuicidal self-injury

- 5 or more days within the last year of intentional self-inflicted damage to the body without suicidal intent
- expectation to relieve negative feelings or thoughts, to resolve a relationship problem or to induce a positive mood

1.2 Definition

As suicidal behaviors are not DSM-5 diagnoses, the diagnostic manual has not been the definitive source for definition and nomenclature that it has been in other areas of mental health. This has caused significant confusion. While many nations do have surveillance systems to monitor deaths by suicide, national surveillance systems for monitoring suicide attempts and estimating national rates of occurrence are far more rare (Silverman et al., 2007a) despite the significance of suicidal behavior as both a clinical and public health issue. In addition, many confusing terms and inconsistencies exist in both the research and clinical literature (Silverman et al., 2007a).

A pivotal event in the development of terminology occurred in 1970 when the Center for the Study of Suicide Prevention of the National Institute of Mental Health convened a committee on classification chaired by Aaron Beck (Brown et al., 2006). A classification system was developed that included the categories of completed suicide, suicide attempts, and suicidal ideation. Suicidal intent was identified as a critical variable in this classification scheme. For a self-injurious behavior to be considered a suicide attempt, suicidal intent was necessary (Beck et al., 1973). Self-injurious behavior was the recommended term when there was no suicidal intent associated with the behavior (Beck et al., 1973).

One challenge for this system has been that suicidal intent, which is essential for determining whether a death by suicide or suicide attempt has occurred, can be very difficult to determine. Self-report on intent after an attempt can be unreliable and heavily influenced by context and the potential consequences for patients of acknowledging suicidal intent. In addition, suicidal intent can

Self-report on suicidal intent can be unreliable and heavily influenced by context and the potential consequences for patients of acknowledging intent to die

Suicidal intent can also fluctuate over time and be fraught with ambivalence

also fluctuate over time and be fraught with ambivalence. Despite these challenges, the nomenclature has met many clinical needs, and terms like suicidal ideation and suicidal intent have become familiar to virtually all clinicians. However, this terminology has proved inadequate for research purposes, leading nomenclature in this field to be described as a "Tower of Babel" (Silverman et al., 2007a) as studies have used varying definitions of terms such as suicide attempt. Such variability in definition has made comparability across studies extremely difficult. In the United Kingdom, the issue of determining intent has been avoided through the use of the term self-harm (formerly deliberate self-harm) (Kapur & Goldney, 2019). This term includes both a suicide attempt as well as nonsuicidal self-injury.

A revised nomenclature has been proposed with support from the Centers for Disease Control and Prevention in the United States (Silverman et al., 2007b). While a key goal of this revision was to help advance research, the revision was also "designed to serve as an instrument to assist clinicians in better identifying those most at risk for suicide related behaviors in order to keep them alive" (Silverman et al., 2007b, p. 274). The revision affirms the crucial role of suicidal intent, and, recognizing the inherently difficult nature of determining intent, utilizes three categories of no intent, uncertain intent, and intent. This replaces the prior dichotomy of suicide attempts vs. self-injury. A suicide attempt is defined as a self-inflicted, potentially injurious behavior with a nonfatal outcome for which there is evidence of intent to die (Silverman et al., 2007b). The term *undetermined suicide-related behavior* is used when suicide intent is uncertain. *Self-harm* is used rather than self-injury when it is clear there is no suicidal intent. This classification system thus explicitly deals with those problematic situations where intent is difficult or impossible to determine.

A suicide plan is a systematic formulation of a program of action with potential to lead to self-injury

Suicide plan is another term frequently used in clinical practice but often not defined clearly. In fact, there is a tendency to equate having a suicide plan with considering a suicide method. While thinking about what method to use in a suicide attempt is clearly subsumed under the notion of planning, by equating them, much important assessment information is often missed. There may be other significant preparatory behaviors taking place (e.g., writing a suicide note, giving away possessions), and simply knowing whether a person has thought of a method tells us nothing about the degree of planning, forethought, and mental rehearsal the person has devoted to the possibility of killing themselves. In this proposed nomenclature, a suicide plan is described more broadly as "a systematic formulation of a program of action that has the potential to lead to self-injury" (Silverman et al., 2007b). An example of systematic planning is provided in Clinical Vignette 1.

The term suicide gesture is pejorative and can lead clinicians to assume the absence of potential lethality prior to a thorough assessment being completed

Another common term in clinical usage is *suicide gesture*. Suicide gesture typically refers to a circumstance in which overt suicidal behavior takes place, but the person's intent is judged by others to be an attempt to communicate distress rather than reflecting true intent to die. These gestures are frequently labeled as manipulative. Such terms are pejorative and can lead clinicians to assume the absence of potential lethality prior to a thorough assessment being completed. The proposed nomenclature recommends against the use of the term suicide gesture because of this pejorative implication (Silverman et al., 2007b). The term should be avoided.

Clinical Vignette 1

Systematic Planning for Suicide

John told several high school friends he was planning on killing himself that night. Alarmed, one of his friends told a parent, who in turn contacted the mental health center. When evaluated, it was discovered that John had obtained a large stash of pills with which to overdose, had given away some of his prized records and other possessions, had decided where he wanted to kill himself, and had picked out the clothes he wanted to be found in when his body was discovered. He exhibited detailed, systematic planning for his suicide. He was assessed as being at high, imminent risk and was hospitalized.

The nomenclature proposed by Silverman and colleagues (2007b) is shown in Table 1. In addition to the important role of suicidal intent, the nomenclature also incorporates whether or not the outcome of a suicidal act is a fatal or nonfatal injury. There can be very serious suicide attempts that do not lead to injury. For example, a person who points a loaded gun at himself and deliberately pulls the trigger has clearly made a suicide attempt, even if the gun jams and there is no resulting injury.

An additional classification system for suicidal events has been proposed by Posner and colleagues (2007). In response to the controversy that swirled around possible links between the use of selective serotonin reuptake inhibitors (SSRIs) and suicidality, the Food and Drug Administration (FDA) commissioned Columbia University to review adverse events involving suicidality in the randomized controlled trials performed by the pharmaceutical companies in the development of the medications. In order to accomplish this, the Columbia Classification Algorithm of Suicide Assessment (C-CASA) was developed, along with the Columbia Suicide Severity Rating Scale (CSSRS). In this system as well, suicidal intent plays a critical role. This system also utilizes terms with significant clinical utility, such as preparatory action toward imminent suicidal behavior, which can include actions such as purchasing pills to overdose or writing a suicide note. This system also utilizes the terms aborted and interrupted suicide attempts. An aborted suicide attempt is when an attempt is stopped by the person themselves, for example, taking out pills or a firearm to use in an attempt and then deciding not to go through with the suicide plan. An interrupted attempt occurs when the attempt is stopped by some other person. In this system, there are essentially four categories rather than the traditional three categories of suicidal ideation, attempts, and deaths by suicide; the fourth category being preparatory behaviors, where the line between ideation and action has been crossed, but short of an action that could cause injury. This system also distinguishes between wish to die without suicidal ideation, specific ideation vs. general ideation, and planning vs. method.

Preparatory suicidal behavior crosses the line between ideation and action

The difference between specific ideation and general ideation is now more typically referred to as the distinction between active and passive suicidal ideation. Passive suicidal ideation is the wish to be dead but without actively thinking about killing oneself. Both forms of suicidal ideation are associated with increased risk thus underscoring how suicide risk occurs on a continuum.

Table 1
Nomenclature for Suicide Related-Behavior

Nomenclature for suicide-related behavior			Intent to die by suicide	Outcomes		
				No injury	Non-fatal injury	Death
Suicide-related behavior	Self-Harm	With no suicidal intent				
		Without injuries self-harm – type I	No	√		
		With injuries self-harm – type II	No		√	
		With fatal injuries self-inflicted unintentional death	No			√
	Undetermined suicide-related behavior	With undetermined suicidal intent				
		Without injuries undetermined suicide-related behavior – type I	Undetermined	√		
		With injuries undetermined suicide-related behavior – type II	Undetermined		√	
		With fatal injuries self-inflicted death with undetermined intent	Undetermined			√
	Suicide Attempt	With suicidal intent				
		Without injuries suicide attempt – type I	Yes	√		
		With injuries suicide attempt – type II	Yes		√	
		With fatal injuries suicide	Yes			√

1.3 Differential Diagnosis

The differential diagnosis of suicide attempts vs. self-harm or nonsuicidal self-injury can be complex for a number of reasons (see Table 2). First, there may be no overt behavioral differences to distinguish between these categories. Rather, the critical difference involves the presence or absence of suicidal intent. If the person tells us that they intended to die when they cut their wrists, we will call it a suicide attempt. If they tell us they did not wish to die, but rather that they were attempting to distract themselves from emotional pain, or to punish themselves, we will call it self-harm, self-mutilation, or nonsuicidal self-injury. In either instance we are relying mostly on the individual's self-report regarding their intent. However, some people who have suicidal intent

Table 2
Differential Diagnosis of Suicide Attempt Versus Self-Harm

Self-Harm (with no suicidal intent) Similar terms: self-mutilation, deliberate self-harm, nonsuicidal self-injury		
	Similarities	**Differences**
Self-harm with no suicidal intent	Intentional act (may result in fatal or nonfatal injuries)	No intent to die (may be a variety of different intents, such as reduce pain, punish self)
Suicide attempt	Intentional act (may result in fatal or nonfatal injuries)	Intent to die

may deny it because of concern they will be hospitalized or because of shame or embarrassment. Others may claim suicidal intent when in reality there was none, feeling that otherwise what they have done may be minimized or invalidated by others. And this distinction presumes that a person was clear at the time of their self-destructive act regarding their intentions. It also presumes they were remembering it clearly, since such acts frequently take place during moments of intense emotional dysregulation (Linehan, 1993).

The following are examples of self-harm with no suicidal intent in Clinical Vignette 2 (nonsuicidal self-injury), a suicide attempt with clear suicidal intent, and a suicide-related behavior with undetermined intent.

Clinical Vignette 2
Role of Suicidal Intent

Self-Harm With No Suicidal Intent (Nonsuicidal Self-Injury)

A physical education teacher noticed during gym class that Julie was trying to conceal multiple cuts on her arms. When interviewed later by the school psychologist, she admitted to cutting herself repeatedly to "relieve my pain." She denied any thoughts about wanting to die or kill herself.

Suicide Attempt With Clear Suicidal Intent

Richard had a long history of depression and alcohol abuse. Following his third arrest for driving while intoxicated, which would trigger the loss of his driver's license, which in turn would force him to quit his job, he took an overdose of approximately 40 of his antidepressants and went to bed, fully expecting he would die in his sleep. In the middle of the night his wife found him stumbling around the bedroom delirious and called 911. When interviewed in the emergency department he reported being upset he was still alive.

Suicide-Related Behavior With Undetermined Intent

Harold was a 31-year-old Caucasian male. Since the onset of legal problems that had been pending over a period of many months, he had been experiencing recurrent suicidal ideation. Intensive outpatient therapy had averted a hospitalization, but he was still being monitored carefully for suicidal risk. While on vacation, he experienced what was presumed to be a serious skiing accident. After a number of days in the hospital for his injuries, he returned to psychotherapy. Since Harold was an excellent skier, his therapist talked with him about how this had happened. Harold acknowledged that he had been having thoughts about suicide that day including as he was getting on the ski lift, but that he had made no plan to kill himself. He reported that as he was skiing down the mountain he went around a curve and left the trail and crashed into a tree at high speed. He did not recall making a conscious decision to try to die. He also didn't know if his wish to die had led him to be less careful and less focused on his safety. He was genuinely uncertain about his suicidal intent.

Presuming to know the meaning or intent of a self-destructive act based on past history and allowing this to bias the assessment is a clinical error

Another complication in making a differential assessment is that the same person may engage at different times in both suicide attempts and self-harm with no suicidal intent. Therefore, each person needs to be assessed without presuming that because they have a history of self-mutilation suicidal intent is not present at the current time. Presuming to know the meaning or intent of a self-destructive act based on past history and allowing this to bias the assessment is a clinical error. Another error in clinical reasoning is to make a judgment about intent based on the degree of lethality of the actions taken. Persons who take an overdose of a few pills or who make superficial cuts should not be presumed to be without suicidal intent based on the lack of lethality of their actions. The person may have misjudged the lethality of their behavior, or may have very serious suicidal intent and be working up the resolve to make a more lethal attempt.

People who make suicide attempts that are low in lethality should not be presumed to be without suicidal intent

The clinician must always assess, not assume

While suicidality and self-harm may seem inextricably interwoven, there are different implications for these two behaviors. Suicide attempts are more likely to lead to psychiatric hospitalization than nonsuicidal self-injury. Self-mutilation is more likely to occur with greater frequency, at times in an almost addictive spiral, compared to suicide attempts. Such distinctions, as well as others, have led Walsh (2006) to argue that the two conditions should be understood, managed, and treated differently. When a person only has a history of self-harm or nonsuicidal self-injury, it is tempting to assume that each repeated episode of harm is unlikely to be a suicide attempt. However, it is hazardous, even for an individual with a history of solely self-harm without suicidal intent, to assume that all future episodes are without suicidal ideation or intent. In a study in England in which patients seen in EDs for episodes of deliberate self-harm were followed up over time, the suicide rate was 36 times that for the general population (Cooper et al., 2005). There was no difference in the suicide rate between those who had reported suicidal intent and those who had not, highlighting the hazard of assuming that those who engage in self-harm without suicidal intent are not at risk for suicide, at least for those whose self-harm is serious enough to warrant emergency care. The clinician must always assess, not assume. Such cases must be managed and assessed considering the potential for suicide risk, at least until the assessment has made clear that there is low risk. An example of the assessment of suicidal intent is provided in Clinical Vignette 3.

Clinical Vignette 3
Assessing Suicidal Intent

Eileen was a 55-year-old, married, Irish-American female with a diagnosis of borderline personality disorder and recurrent major depressions. She was referred to the clinic for dialectical behavior therapy. She had a history of many episodes of self-harm without suicidal intent, as well as several suicide attempts, some utilizing potentially lethal methods such as hanging. During the course of treatment, she made additional suicide attempts and there were episodes of self-harm without suicidal intent, although the frequency of such episodes declined over time with continuing treatment. Assessment around these episodes revealed that there were times that there was clear suicidal intent, there were times that suicidal intent was clearly absent, and there were times that in the throes of emotional dysregulation, Eileen was simply unsure what her intent had been.

1.4 Epidemiology

The epidemiology of suicidal behavior, particularly deaths by suicide, has been studied extensively, both in the US as well as in many countries around the world. In 2019, there were an estimated 700,000 suicides worldwide, including 173,347 deaths by suicide in India, and more than 116,324 in China (WHO, 2021). However, to fully understand the impact that suicidality represents to our society, as well as to nations around the world, it is important to understand the different levels of suicidal behavior that exist, including deaths by suicide, suicide attempts, and suicidal thinking, and the burdens these impose, including the costs of hospitalizations and ED visits.

The number of suicides in the United States has been steadily increasing year after year, exceeding 48,000 suicides in 2018. Significantly more Americans die by suicide than by homicide, by a 3:2 ratio. According to the most recent data available from the Centers for Disease Control and Prevention (CDC, 2021), suicide is the tenth leading cause of death for all ages, accounting for 1.73% of all deaths in the United States (see Table 3). Suicide is the eighth leading cause of death among males, accounting for 2.6% of male deaths. For some age groups, suicide ranks even higher as a leading cause of death. Suicide is the second leading cause of death for ages 10–34 years. The more than 48,000 suicides that occurred in the US in 2018 equates to a rate of 14.5 suicides per 100,000 population (CDC, 2021). On average, an American dies by suicide every 11 minutes.

On average, an American dies by suicide every 11 minutes

Males outnumber females in suicide deaths by a ratio of 3.5:1. However, suicide in the United States has been rising among both males and females, among all age groups, and among all races, with the highest rates among those ages 45–64 years and above age 85, particularly among males.

These increases, along with increases in deaths by accidental overdoses, particularly opioids, and in alcohol involved liver disease have led to a decrease in life expectancy in the United States for 3 consecutive years, the first time this has happened since the great flu epidemic a century ago (Woolf & Schoomaker, 2019). The economists Case and Deaton characterized these as the deaths of despair (Case & Deaton, 2017), and they noted that this pattern differs from what is happening in other industrialized nations such as England, Scotland, and Japan (WHO, 2014).

Firearms are the most commonly used method of suicide in the United States

Firearms are the most commonly used method of suicide in the United States accounting for 50.6% of all suicides. Rural areas have higher suicide rates than urban and suburban areas and the gap between them has been widening over time.

In the United States, suicide risk is highest among Caucasians, American Indians, and Alaska Natives. American Indian and Alaska Native youth and young adults have particularly high suicide rates. Increases in suicide have also been reported among indigenous people internationally including the Canadian Inuit, New Zealand Maori, and Australian Aboriginal people (Kapur & Goldney, 2019). For both fatal and nonfatal self-harm, injury rates begin to rise sharply at ages 13 and 14 years (Vajani et al., 2007). This pattern has been found internationally as well by Nock and colleagues (2008).

Clinicians need to be aware of the hazards of adapting epidemiologic data to clinical practice without careful analysis. Assigning risk to groups in the population tends to be interpreted in relation to the US average, but it is critical to remember that even if a group has a lower suicide rate than the national average this does not mean that hundreds, if not thousands, from that demographic group may not die by suicide every year. For example, the fact that significantly more males than females die by suicide does not mean that clinicians should not be alert to suicide risk in women. In fact, more than 50% of female suicides occur among those receiving mental health treatment (CDC, 2008), underscoring the importance for clinicians of being alert to the potential for suicide in women. While suicide in the United States has been increasing among both men and women, the percentage increase has been greater among females.

The epidemiology of suicide attempts differs in important respects from deaths by suicide. A significant advance in suicide attempt surveillance occurred in 2008 when the Substance Abuse and Mental Health Services Administration added to the National Survey on Drug Use and Health (NSDUH) questions about suicidal ideation, plans, attempts, and attempts requiring medical attention. This extensive household survey has allowed national estimates to be generated every year. In 2020, NSDUH estimated that 1.2 million Americans attempted suicide and over 12 million American adults age 18 years and older seriously considered suicide (Substance Abuse and Mental Health Services Administration, 2021). In a study by the Agency for Healthcare Research and Quality, ED visits related to suicidal ideation among adults age 18 years and over increased by an average of 12% per year from 2006 to 2013, nearly doubling to a total of 900,000 ED visits. Over 70% of these visits resulted in hospitalization (Owens et al., 2017). Similarly, a study of youth ages 10–18 years presenting to EDs for suicidal ideation or attempts also showed a doubling from 2007 to 2015 (Burstein et al., 2019).

The ratio of deaths by suicide to suicide attempts varies dramatically with age. Among young adults ages 15–24 years, there is 1 suicide for every 100–200 attempts (Institute of Medicine et al., 2002). Among adults ages 65 years and older, there is 1 suicide for every 4 suicide attempts (Institute of Medicine et al., 2002).

Table 3
10 Leading Causes of Death by Age Group, United States – 2017

	Age Groups										
Rank	<1	1–4	5–9	10–14	15–24	25–34	35–44	45–54	55–65	65+	Total
1	Congenital Anomalies 4,473	Unintentional Injury 1,226	Unintentional Injury 734	Unintentional Injury 692	Unintentional Injury 12,044	Unintentional Injury 24,614	Unintentional Injury 22,667	Malignant Neoplasms 37,3001	Malignant Neoplasms 113,947	Heart Disease 526,509	Heart Disease 655,381
2	Short Gestation 3,679	Congenital Anomalies 384	Malignant Neoplasms 393	Suicide 596	Suicide 6,211	Suicide 8,020	Malignant Neoplasms 10,640	Heart Disease 32,220	Heart Disease 81,042	Malignant Neoplasms 431,102	Malignant Neoplasms 599,274
3	Maternal Pregnancy Comp. 1,358	Homicide 353	Congenital Anomalies 201	Malignant Neoplasms 450	Homicide 4,607	Homicide 5,234	Heart Disease 10,532	Unintentional Injury 23,056	Unintentional Injury 23,693	Chronic Low. Respiratory Disease 135,560	Unintentional Injury 167,127
4	SIDS 1,334	Malignant Neoplasms 326	Homicide 121	Congenital Anomalies 172	Malignant Neoplasms 1,371	Malignant Neoplasms 3,684	Suicide 7,521	Suicide 8,345	Chronic Low. Respiratory Disease 18,804	Cerebrovascular 127,244	Chronic Low. Respiratory Disease 159,486
5	Unintentional Injury 1,168	Influenza & Pneumonia 122	Influenza & Pneumonia 71	Homicide 168	Heart Disease 905	Heart Disease 3,561	Homocide 3,304	Liver Disease 8,157	Diabetes Mellitus 14,941	Alzheimer's Disease 120,658	Cerebrovascular 147,810
6	Placenta Cord Membranes 724	Heart Disease 115	Chronic Low. Respiratory Disease 68	Heart Disease 101	Congenital Anomalies 354	Liver Disease 1,008	Liver Disease 3,108	Diabetes Mellitus 6,414	Liver Disease 13,945	Diabetes Mellitus 60,182	Alzheimer's Disease 122,019
7	Bacterial Sepsis 579	Perinatal Period 62	Heart Disease 68	Chronic Low. Respiratory Disease 64	Diabetes Mellitus 246	Diabetes Mellitus 837	Diabetes Mellitus 2,282	Cerebrovascular 5,128	Cerebrovascular 12,789	Unintentional Injury 57,213	Diabetes Mellitus 84,946
8	Circulatory System Disease 428	Septicemia 54	Cerebrovascular 34	Cerebrovascular 54	Influenza & Pneumonia 200	Cerebrovascular 567	Cerebrovascular 1,704	Chronic Low. Respiratory Disease 3,807	Suicide 8,540	Influenza & Pneumonia 48,888	Influenza & Pneumonia 59,120
9	Respiratory Disease 390	Chronic Low. Respiratory Disease 50	Septicemia 34	Influenza & Pneumonia 51	Chronic Low. Respiratory Disease 165	HIV 482	Influenza & Pneumonia 956	Septicemia 2,380	Septicemia 5,956	Nephritis 42,232	Nephritis 51,386
10	Neonatal Hemorrhage 375	Cerebrovascular 43	Benign Neoplasms 19	Benign Neoplasms 30	Complicated Pregnancy 151	Influenza & Pneumonia 457	Septicemia 829	Influenza & Pneumonia 2,339	Influenza & Pneumonia 5.858	Parkinson's Disease 32,988	Suicide 48,344

Source: National Vital Statistics System, National Center for Health Statistics, CDC. Produced by: Office of Statistics and Programming. National Center for Injury Prevention and Control, CDC, using WISQARS. Available at https://www.cdc.gov/injury/wisqars/pdf/leading_causes_of_death_by_age_group_2017-508.pdf

Other estimates of suicide attempts come from the Youth Risk Behavior Survey (YRBS), a US, school-based survey conducted by the Centers for Disease Control and Prevention that utilizes a self-report instrument. YRBS monitors risk behaviors that contribute to the leading causes of death, disability, and social problems among youth in the United States (see Table 4). The YRBS is conducted every 2 years and provides data representative of 9th–12th grade students in public and private schools throughout the United States.

In 2017, 17.2% of students in grades 9–12 had seriously considered suicide in the previous 12 months (22.1% of females and 11.9% of males; Kann et al., 2018). In that year, 7.4% of students reported making at least one suicide attempt (9.3% of females and 5.1% of males) while 2.4% of students reported making at least one suicide attempt in the previous 12 months that required medical attention (3.1% of females and 1.5% of males; Kann et al., 2018). Based on these findings, it appears that a significant majority of those who attempt suicide, at least among youth, never come to the attention of the healthcare system.

Recent major advances in knowledge have resulted from the implementation of the National Violent Death Reporting System (NVDRS). The system began in 17 states but has now expanded to all 50 states. Operated in coordination with the Centers for Disease Control and Prevention, the NVDRS is able to provide statewide data on characteristics of people who die by suicide that were previously not available because most data on deaths by suicide were derived from death certificates. Death certificates only contain basic information such as age, sex, race, and cause of death. Hence, we have not had systematic epidemiological data on questions such as the prevalence of suicide among military veterans, the frequency of homicide/suicides, or how often those who have died by suicide have received prior mental health treatment. By linking death certificate data with data from police reports and laboratory findings, our knowledge is being substantially enhanced. For example, we now estimate that approximately 14% of those who die by suicide are either current or former US military personnel, that combined homicide/suicides occur most frequently in the context of domestic violence, and that only 23% of men but 40% of women were currently receiving mental health treatment (Ertl et al., 2019).

Table 4
YRBS Suicidal Thoughts and Behavior: Students 9–12th Grade (2019)

Thoughts and behavior	Percentage of total
Seriously considered suicide in the previous 12 months	18.8%
Made at least one suicide attempt in the past 12 months	8.9%
Made at least one suicide attempt in the past 12 months that required medical attention	2.5%

Source: CDC, 2020

1.5 Course and Prognosis

Suicide is not a disorder per se with a clear course and prognosis. The course varies depending on whether one is analyzing populations having suicidal thoughts, those making suicide attempts, or those who have died by suicide. The pattern differs still if one is examining those disorders that are associated with increased suicide risk, such as affective disorders, substance abuse, or personality disorders. Yet some conclusions can be drawn.

First, suicide is never inevitable. No matter how high the risk for an individual, no matter how deep and realistic the clinician's level of concern, there is always hope. The absence of hope on the part of a clinician that a patient can survive his or her suicidal impulses is a powerful signal of the need for consultation.

A clinician who feels hopeless that a patient can survive their suicidal impulses needs to obtain a consultation

The epidemiology is clear: Many more people think about suicide than act on those thoughts. And, of those who act on those thoughts, many more make nonfatal suicide attempts than die by suicide. While all those who make either fatal or nonfatal suicide attempts must have previously thought about it, not all those who die by suicide have made a previous attempt. Maris has estimated that 30% of those who die by suicide progress from thought to nonfatal suicidal behavior to fatal suicidal behavior (Maris, 1992). In a Finnish study, 44% of those who died by suicide were found to have had a previous suicide attempt, with females being more likely to have a previous suicide attempt compared to males (Isometsa & Lonnqvist, 1998). In the United States, data from the National Violent Death Reporting System indicated 19.9% of suicide decedents had a known previous suicide attempt (Kann et al., 2018). The true number is likely to be higher as not all suicide attempts are known to police, coroners or medical examiners, or even family members. On the basis of hospital admitted or treated populations, individuals who have self-harmed have a 30–200-fold increase in risk compared to individuals who have not self-harmed (Cooper et al., 2005). Kapur and Goldney (2019) estimate that those who self-harm are at least 30 times more likely to die by suicide during the following year than the general population. A review of the international literature (Carroll et al., 2014) found that in the year following self-harm the incidence of suicide was 1.6% and of repeat self-harm was 16.3%.

30–40% of those who die by suicide progress from thoughts, to nonfatal suicidal behavior, to fatal suicidal behavior

In a recent study, the standardized mortality ratio for those seen in EDs for a suicide attempt was 56:8 (Goldman-Mellor et al., 2019).

Those who self-harm are at least 30 times more likely to die by suicide during the following year. When seen in an ED for a suicide attempt, the risk was 56 times greater

For others who make suicide attempts, some will never again engage in suicidal behavior while some will make subsequent, multiple additional attempts but not die by suicide. Maris (1981) estimated that approximately 15% of suicide attempters go on to die by suicide. The critical trajectory is thus from suicidal thoughts to suicidal behavior.

Suicidal ideation is relatively common. The 2019 YRBS showed that more than 18% of youths reported seriously considering suicide within the last year (CDC, 2020). The NSDUH (2006) showed that 40% of adults with major depressive episodes wanted to kill themselves during their worst or most recent episode, and 10% made suicide attempts (Substance Abuse and Mental Health Services Administration, 2006). According to the 2015 NSDUH, 28.6% of those with a major depression in the past year seriously considered suicide (Piscopo et al., 2016). Thus, thoughts about killing oneself are almost

Prior to 2008, NSDUH asked only those with major depression about suicide. Since 2008, national estimates of suicidal thoughts, plans, and attempts may be generated for adults from NSDUH surveys

normative for those suffering from major depression; however, only a minority will take the next step and engage in suicidal behavior.

When one examines the topography of suicidal thoughts and scrutinizes the full continuum of these phenomena, from a passive longing for death to suicidal intent and plans, a clear intensification can be seen. As Shneidman (1996) describes it, "The mind scans its options: the topic of suicide comes up, the mind rejects it, scans again, there is suicide, it is rejected again, and then finally the mind accepts suicide as a solution, then plans it, then fixes on it as the only answer" (p. 15). The same person at the end of this process is clearly more at risk than at the start. Though both can be described as having suicidal ideation, the person at the end of this process has suicidal ideation, suicidal intent, and a suicide plan. Jamison (1999) puts this same process in more evocative language, "If it has ever been taken up as an option, the black knight has a tendency to remain in play" (p. 4).

While it is clear that suicidal thoughts can intensify in terms of frequency and duration, and that planning for suicide can become more elaborate and more specific, more research is needed to describe how these processes develop into lethal actions. There is also a need for more research helping us understand how a person develops suicidal intent, where there is not only thinking about suicide, but also "a resolve to act" (Silverman et al., 2007a).

Thoughts about killing oneself are almost normative for those suffering from major depression

There is evidence that the prevalence of suicide planning more closely resembles suicide attempts than suicidal ideation. Among those with major depressive episodes, 56.3% thought during their worst or most recent episode that they would be better off dead, 40.3% thought about dying by suicide, while 14.5% made a suicide plan, and 10.4% made an attempt (Substance Abuse and Mental Health Services Administration, 2006).

60% of the transitions from ideation to first suicide attempt occurred within the first year since the onset of suicidal ideation

While there is frequently a long period between the initial onset of suicidal ideation and suicidal behavior, the pathway from ideation to attempt can be rapid once active planning and preparatory behaviors begin to take place

The next step, once the "black knight" is in play, is moving from thought to action, from considering self- destruction to attempting it. In a cross-national study, 60% of the transitions from suicidal ideation to first suicide attempt occurred within the first year since the onset of suicidal ideation (Nock et al., 2008). In a study of suicidal ideators who went on to make suicide attempts over a 12-month period, those who had made a suicide plan were significantly more likely to make a suicide attempt than those who had not made a plan (Borges et al., 2006). The progression from suicidal thoughts to suicidal behavior is now a major focus of suicide prevention theory and research (Joiner, 2005; Klonsky & May, 2015; O'Connor, 2011). In a small but important study, Milner and colleagues (2017) attempted to describe and measure the pathway from suicidal ideation to a suicide attempt. They found that although the median onset for suicidal ideation occurs 1–5 years before attempting suicide, continuous suicidal ideation only began 2 weeks prior to the attempt. They further found that the onset of thoughts about where to attempt suicide occurred 1 week prior while mulling or seriously considering suicide occurred 6 hours prior to the attempt. Certainty about method occurred 2 hours prior to the attempt and certainty about where to attempt suicide 30 minutes before the attempt. The final decision to make the attempt occurred 5 minutes before the attempt. No one in the study had made the decision more than 3 days previously. While there is frequently a long period between the initial onset of suicidal ideation and suicidal behavior, the pathway from ideation to attempt can be rapid once active planning and preparatory behaviors begin to take place.

Since over their lifetimes, on average, only 15% of those who make a nonfatal suicide attempt eventually go on to kill themselves (Maris, 1992), a suicide attempt is certainly not an inevitable harbinger of death by suicide. However, since 30–40% of those who ultimately die by suicide have made a previous attempt, this makes a prior suicide attempt the single strongest risk factor for death by suicide (Hawton, 2005). However, there is significant variation by age and gender. For example, Maris (1992) reports that 88% of males above age 45 years made only a single, fatal attempt while among youth suicide attempts greatly outnumber deaths by suicide.

A prior suicide attempt is the single strongest risk factor for death by suicide

In addition, those who make suicide attempts vary in the number of suicide attempts made. In a survey by Maris (1992), of those who died by suicide and had made a prior suicide attempt, 70% had made one prior attempt, approximately 14% had made two previous attempts, and the rest had made three attempts or more.

Additional research has further demonstrated the significant mortality and morbidity associated with suicide attempts. In a five-year follow-up, Beautrais (2004) found that of 302 individuals who made a medically serious suicide attempt, almost half (44.5%) either made another suicide attempt or died by suicide. The mortality rate from suicide over that 5-year period was 6.7% while more than 37% made an additional nonfatal suicide attempt. Those who made additional suicide attempts were more likely to have made a suicide attempt in the 5 years prior to the index attempt and to have had a psychiatric admission in the previous year (Beautrais, 2004). Of particular significance, Beautrais also found that among those who died by suicide, a significant number (75%) changed from the method used at the index attempt to a more lethal method that resulted in their death. This is strong evidence that many who die by suicide escalate the lethality of their actions over time, a point emphasized in recent work by Joiner (2005), who argues that people who die by suicide must acquire the capacity to inflict lethal self-harm by becoming gradually desensitized to this fearsome behavior.

Many who died by suicide utilized increasingly lethal methods in comparison to the index attempt

Beautrais argues that those who attempt suicide should receive intensive follow-up services, particularly in light of the difficulty in identifying characteristics that would predict later death. The only such characteristic to be identified was, in the immediate aftermath of the attempt, the person attempting suicide regretted survival and still wanted to die.

Regretting surviving a suicide attempt should be considered a very important sign of future risk

In a prospective cohort study of 7,968 ER patients seen for deliberate self-harm, the suicide rate in the following year was 371 per 100,000, approximately 34 times the expected rate (Cooper et al., 2005). Suicide rates were highest within the next 6 months following the index self-harm episode. Independent predictors of subsequent suicide were engaging in efforts to avoid discovery at the time of the episode, alcohol misuse, and not living with close relatives. Whether the self-injury was intended as a suicide attempt was not a significant predictor of subsequent suicide in this study.

While some will make a suicide attempt and never attempt again, others will make further attempts, escalating in lethality, until ultimately death by suicide occurs. It is of critical importance that those who make multiple suicide attempts be viewed as a very high-risk population in need of intensive treatment. In the study of Beautrais (2004), over a quarter (26.2%) made four or more attempts within a five-year period. These findings rebut the stereotype that those who make multiple suicide attempts are not "seriously" suicidal and engage only in low lethality suicidal behavior. At the same time, the absence of this kind of history of suicidal behavior cannot be viewed as assurance that someone is not at risk for suicide. Particularly among older persons, the first suicide attempt may be fatal.

When examining those who have attempted suicide without regard to the lethality of the attempt, Owens and colleagues (2002) found that 23% had made further attempts and 3.4% had died by suicide upon four-year follow-up. Gibb and colleagues (2005), when looking at hospitalized suicide attempters regardless of lethality level, found 28.1% were re-admitted for a further suicide attempt, and 4.6% died by suicide, leading these researchers to the conclusion that the risk of subsequent suicide and further suicide attempts following an index suicide attempt is higher for all those who attempt suicide, regardless of the medical severity of the attempt.

An important contribution to the literature on the circumstances preceding lethal and near lethal suicidal behavior was the Houston Case Control Study of Nearly Lethal Suicide Attempts (Simon et al., 2001) This study found that up to 24% of nearly lethal suicide attempters had spent less than 5 minutes between the decision to attempt suicide and the actual nearly lethal suicide attempt. In fact, 5% reported spending only one second (Simon et al., 2001). The association of these near-lethal impulsive suicide attempts with physical fighting, particularly among males, suggests a potential role of intense emotional dysregulation. While on the surface the findings of Simon et al. (2001) may make it seem that many suicide attempts "come out of the blue" and are spontaneous, impulsive acts, it is quite possible that such impulsive acts were actually preceded by a period of thinking and planning that ultimately reached an apparently sudden "tipping point" (Goldney, 1998). The fact that approximately one third of these impulsive, near lethal attempters reported telling someone that they were considering suicide (Simon et al., 2001) supports this notion. For the entire sample of persons making near lethal suicide attempts, 48% had sought help from family or friends (Barnes et al., 2001) in the month prior to the attempt. Of these, 43% discussed suicide, underscoring the importance for clinicians of involving family and significant others in treatment. The rate at which persons who made near-lethal attempts sought help from professionals was less than from family and friends. In this study, 37% sought help from a professional, and of these 41% discussed suicide, suggesting the need for improved intervention by professionals. Thus, suicide does not typically come out of the blue, but rather following a period of contemplation and desensitization to the idea of suicide, which can then rapidly intensify to suicidal action.

Approx. one third of people who made impulsive, nearly lethal suicide attempts reported they told someone they were considering suicide

1.6 Comorbidities

The most significant comorbidities impacting suicide risk are comorbid mood disorders and substance abuse. Each is its own independent risk factor for suicide. Depression and hopelessness have been found to be strongly correlated with death by suicide (Beck et al., 1989). In a national long-term follow-up study of suicide risk following first psychiatric contact in Denmark, the absolute lifetime risk for suicide in bipolar disorder was 7.8% for males and 4.8% for females. For patients with unipolar depression the figures were 6.7% for males and 3.8% for females (Nordentoft et al., 2011). For patients with mood disorders, a recent suicide attempt combined with severe major depression is particularly alarming (Rihmer et al., 2015).

The most significant comorbidities impacting suicide risk are mood disorders and substance abuse

The relationship between depression and suicidality is one of the most critical conceptual issues in the field of suicide prevention. Suicide can be viewed as the most tragic outcome of untreated depression and as an expression of depression at its most severe. The finding from the National Survey on Drug Use and Health that almost 40% of those with major depression reported seriously considering suicide in the past year underscores further the close relationship between clinical depression and suicidal ideation (Piscopo et al., 2016). For this reason, for many years treatment of depression has been considered synonymous with treatment for suicide risk. However, it has become clear that treatments for depression, particularly psychotherapies, that do not include a focus on what is driving thinking about suicide are less likely to reduce risk. Similarly, screening for depression without also screening for suicide risk has been shown to be less effective, as suicide is clearly related to a wide range of mental disorders besides depression or mood disorders.

An additional concern is the finding by Copeland and colleagues (2017) that suicidal ideation in adolescents, when combined with depression, is more associated with adult suicidal thoughts and behaviors. While one in ten youth with suicidal ideation without depression had suicidal thoughts or behavior as adults, one in two youth with suicidal ideation and depression had suicidal thoughts or behavior as an adult.

Suicidal ideation in adolescents, when combined with depression, is associated with adult suicidal thoughts and behaviors

Besides depression and mood disorders, the conditions most associated with suicide are substance use and abuse. Of deaths by suicide, 37% have been found to have alcohol present at the time of death (Cherpitel et al., 2004). The presence of substance abuse also makes it more difficult to accept patients' statements that they are not going to attempt to kill themselves. A patient may be able to assure us they are not suicidal when they are sober, but the lack of suicidal ideation or intent while sober may be a poor predictor of the likelihood of suicidal behavior when intoxicated.

Lack of suicidal ideation and intent while sober may be a poor predictor of suicidal behavior while intoxicated

The IOM estimated that about one fourth of all the suicides in the United States are individuals with alcohol use disorders (Institute of Medicine et al., 2002). Estimates of substance use disorder in other countries range from 7% in China to 61% in Estonia (Conner & Bagge, 2019). Without question, more research has been done on the relationship of alcohol to suicidal behavior than any other drug. Increasingly however, as deaths from opioid overdose have continued to rise dramatically, more research on the relationship between opioid use and abuse is being done.

In a rigorous review of published studies that evaluated acute alcohol use at the time of death by suicide, Cherpitel and colleagues (2004) found that toxicology screening and blood alcohol concentration measurements averaged 37% for acute alcohol use. In 16 studies of suicide attempts and acute alcohol use, most of which were conducted in hospital EDs, an average of 40% had acute alcohol use (Cherpitel et al., 2004). Thus, for both death by suicide and suicide attempts, acute alcohol use played a role in over one third of the cases, a finding of great clinical significance. A recent meta-analysis of the acute use of alcohol and the risk of suicide attempt found that acute use of alcohol is associated with increased likelihood of a suicide attempt, particularly at high doses (Borges et al., 2017).

Acute alcohol use can intensify suicidal ideation

There are several possible mechanisms by which acute alcohol use might make suicidal behavior more likely. A state of intoxication may trigger self-inflicted injuries by intensifying depressive thoughts or feelings of hopelessness while simultaneously lessening inhibitions to hurting oneself (Skog, 1991). Acute alcohol use can intensify suicidal ideation and can also be used to deliberately facilitate an attempt, for example, by numbing fears about making a suicide attempt (Bagge et al., 2015) There have been efforts to study the relationship more systematically than is possible in simple cross-sectional designs by using a case-crossover study design. Data obtained in this manner have suggested that any acute alcohol use increases the risk of suicide attempts, not only alcohol use that exceeds the legal limits for intoxication (Cherpitel et al., 2004). Of particular significance, a recent study by Bagge and colleagues (2014) found that during the 24 hours prior to a suicide attempt the acute alcohol use during an hour led to increased intensity of suicidal ideation in the subsequent hour.

Binge drinking episodes have been found to frequently precede serious suicide attempts (Moscicki, 2001) and death by suicide. While binge drinking has a proximal effect on suicidal behavior, general alcohol consumption also had a significant impact over time. Level of general alcohol use predicted suicidal ideation, suicidal communications, and suicide attempts, even when depression and past suicidal behavior were controlled for.

On the basis of an empirical review of cohort studies, Inskip and colleagues (1998) estimated that 7% of alcoholics die by suicide, as compared to their estimate that 6% of those with affective disorders kill themselves. Conner and Duberstein (2004), analyzing retrospective, postmortem studies, found that 34–56% met criteria for alcohol abuse or dependence. They also examined predisposing and precipitating factors for suicide among alcoholics and attempted a conceptual integration to help inform future research, clinical interventions, and prevention efforts. They propose that aggression/impulsivity, alcoholism severity, and hopelessness are predisposing factors that distinguish alcoholics who are at heightened risk for suicide (see Box 2). Suicide among alcoholics frequently takes place within the context of a major depression and interpersonal stressors, which play some role for suicide in general, but likely play a particularly important role for suicide among alcoholics, particularly partner disruptions.

Alcoholism and depression are frequently comorbid. Postmortem case control studies have shown that rates of depression are higher in alcoholics who died by suicide compared to control groups of alcoholic and substance use disorders (Conner et al., 2003). Studies have shown major depression to be present at the end of life for suicide decedents with alcohol and substance use disorders in the range of 45% (Conner et al., 1999) to over 70% (Cheng, 1995). However, the elevated rate of suicide among alcoholics is not simply due to the elevated base rate of depression in this population (Conner & Duberstein, 2004).

The temporal relationship between alcoholism and depression and the nature of their relationship in death by suicide is not entirely clear (Conner & Duberstein, 2004). In some studies, alcoholism was found to precede depression in adults (Cheng, 1995; Murphy et al., 1979) while a case control study of suicide in adolescents reached the opposite conclusion. In their study of youths, Brent and colleagues (1993a) found that depression was more likely to precede substance abuse. There may well be a sex difference in this regard, at least among adults. While studies such as that of Murphy and Robbins (1967) found alcoholism preceding depression in males, depression is more likely to precede alcoholism among females who die by suicide (Pirkola et al., 1999), a finding consistent with studies that show a general trend for depression to be more likely to precede alcoholism in women than in men (Schuckit et al., 1997).

Box 2
Risk Factors for Suicidal Behavior Among Alcoholics

Aggression/impulsivity
Alcoholism severity
Hopelessness
Negative affect/episode of major depression
Partner-relationship disruptions

A general tendency to experience negative affect has been demonstrated to precede the development of major depression, the recurrence of depression and the persistence of depressive symptoms, and is associated with depression in treated substance abusers (Conner & Duberstein, 2004). There may be a subgroup of alcoholics whose depression precedes their alcoholism, and whose drinking is an attempt to cope with their negative affect, who may be at heightened risk of suicide compared to other alcoholics (Preuss et al., 2002).

Partner-related disruptions may be especially important in suicides by those with alcohol and substance abuse disorders

Partner-related disruptions may be particularly important in suicide in alcoholics (Conner & Duberstein, 2004). This finding was first demonstrated in the groundbreaking study of Murphy and Robbin (1967) that showed disruptions in interpersonal relationships occurred more frequently among alcoholics who died by suicide than among any other diagnostic group. A recent case control investigation comparing alcoholics who died by suicide and alcoholic community controls showed that both partner-relationship disruptions and other interpersonal difficulties, including difficulties with other family members, were independent risk factors for suicide (Conner et al., 2003). Similarly, a controlled postmortem study in adolescents who died by suicide found that interpersonal loss, most frequently a break up with a boyfriend or girlfriend, was more common in youths with substance abuse disorders than in youths with mood or conduct disorders who also died by suicide (Brent et al., 1993b). Conner and Duberstein (2004) make a point that is of particular importance for clinicians, "The proximity of interpersonal disruptions to suicide also hints at their importance, as they tend to cluster in the last 6 weeks of life in individuals with alcohol or substance abuse disorders" (p. 11).

Aggression and impulsivity may be linked to alcoholism severity. Conner and Duberstein (2004) propose a model that utilizes the construct of reactive aggression. Reactive aggression refers to impulsive, angry responses to aversive events. With more chronic alcohol use patterns, relationships may become more conflictual, with the alcohol use itself a significant source of conflict. More aversive interactions lead to increased impulsive, angry responses. Such individuals may display a pattern of emotional dysregulation and be prone to distressing, interpersonal situations, including inadvertently eliciting rejection by others. Thus, emotional dysregulation, particularly relationship damaging outbursts of anger or hostility, cause interpersonal turmoil and exacerbate depression and hopelessness, intensifying suicide risk.

While far more research has examined the role of alcohol in suicidal behavior than any other drug, the National Violent Death Reporting System (Karch et al., 2006) demonstrated that a variety of different drugs were present at the time of suicide. While 33.3% of suicide decedents tested positive for alcohol, 16.4% tested positive for opiates, 9.4% tested positive for cocaine, 7.7% tested positive for marijuana, and 3.9% tested positive for amphetamines. Because of the alarming and tragic increases in fatal opioid overdoses in the United States, increasing attention has been given to the relationship between opioid use and abuse, and suicidal ideation, attempts and deaths. CDC mortality data from 2017 shows suicide and unintentional opioid overdose deaths to be equivalent scourges with 47,700 opioid deaths and 47,100 suicides, in 2017, with both increasing.

Opioid use disorders appear to have a stronger relationship to suicide than do other substance use disorders other than alcohol (Bohnert & Ilgen, 2019). The role of pain is likely significant in this association. Chronic pain diagnoses are linked to suicide, and this relationship is only partly explained by co-occurring mental health conditions (Bohnert & Ilgen, 2019). A study in the US Department of Veterans Affairs showed an association between higher prescribed dosage of opioids and higher rates of suicide deaths (Ilgen et al., 2016). Some opioid overdose deaths are in fact suicides, but it can be difficult to make this determination, which is based on the persons intent, unless a suicide note has been left. Patients sometimes report that they cannot differentiate whether an overdose was a suicide attempt or accidental. Also, when a given patient survives an overdose their perceived intent may change in retrospect. Clinically, patients with substance use disorders should be given particular attention for the prevention of both suicide and overdose, with the risk of both likely to be highest when there is comorbid depression and substance use disorder. Of interest is that the use of antidepressants in this population has been shown to reduce the risk of overdose among patients with depression using opioid analgesics.

Mortality risk for both suicide and accidental overdose are markedly elevated in the 12 months following an ED visit for suicidal ideation/suicide attempt

Additionally, risk scores that calculate a specific patient's level of risk for suicide, overdose or both have been developed based on data from electronic health records, and have been implemented nationally by the US Department of Veterans Affairs. In a recently published study that examined mortality in the year after being seen in an ED for either a suicide attempt or suicidal ideation, risk was elevated both for suicide as well as for accidental overdose death further underscoring the close relationship (Goldman-Mellor et al., 2019). In addition, in a parallel study the researchers found significant elevations for both accidental overdose deaths and suicides in the 12 months following an ED visit for a nonfatal accidental overdose (Goldman-Mellor et al., 2020).

Bohnert and Ilgen (2019) summarize the research on medication assisted therapy, which is the combination of medications such as Methadone or Naloxone with counseling for opioid use disorders, as reducing overdose mortality, potentially impacting both intentional and unintentional overdose. However, some deaths still continue and the risks of death are highest when medication is initiated and when the treatment suddenly stops. This is consistent with the findings in suicide research of increased risks during any transitions in care. Finally, it is unclear whether opioid tapering reduces suicide mortality by decreasing access to lethal means, or increases it by resulting in poorly controlled pain increasing suicidality. It is also possible that the anticipation of tapering leading to uncontrolled pain could lead to suicidal ideation in some individuals.

There is emerging evidence that the greatest risk for suicide in those diagnosed with schizophrenia is early in the disorder

Lifetime risk of suicide in those diagnosed with schizophrenia is also significantly elevated and is currently estimated to be about 5%. There is emerging evidence that the greatest risk for suicide is early on in the course of the disorder (Desîlets et al., 2016). Prior to their first treatment, up to 14–38% of those with first-episode psychosis had already attempted suicide (Melle & Barrett, 2012). As efforts to intervene as soon as possible in first-episode psychosis have been increasing internationally, the potential that suicidal ideation or attempts could be a marker for developing psychosis in a certain vulnerable subgroup should be kept in mind. Detecting suicidal ideation in this group could serve the purpose both of keeping the person safe but also intervening earlier in their episode which increases the likelihood of a successful recovery. The importance of this is highlighted in a historical control study to support the potential association of an early intervention service with reduction in suicide during a 12-year period, with the maximum association during the first 3 years (Chan et al., 2018).

Risk of suicide in personality disorder, particularly borderline personality disorder is also elevated, as well as the risk for repeated nonfatal suicidal behavior (Paris, 2019). Too often suicidal behavior or suicidal communications by people with borderline personality disorder are seen as manipulative. And not reflective of actual risk. It is essential for all clinicians to recognize that the risk of suicide in borderline personality disorder is very real and should not be minimized.

The relationship between suicidal behavior and trauma is an important, emerging area, and a 2002 IOM report emphasized the role of trauma in the development of suicidality (Institute of Medicine et al., 2002). The most comprehensive, longitudinal study of pathways to suicide was conducted in New Zealand and followed 1,265 adolescents. The study found that child sexual abuse, parental alcoholism, and poor attachment to parents were predictive of suicide attempts by age 21 years, with much of the relationship mediated by mental illness and stressful life events (Fergusson et al., 2000). However, in the National Comorbidity Study, Molnar and colleagues (2001) found that while the majority of suicide attempts were attributable to mental disorder, a significant number of suicide attempts occurred in the absence of psychopathology. The IOM report also concluded that sexual abuse was the strongest and most important risk factor for suicide attempts, accounting for 9–20% of all suicide attempts (Institute of Medicine et al., 2002). Beautrais (2004) found childhood adversity closely linked to repeated suicidal behavior, although not with death by suicide. In the United States, the Adverse Childhood Experiences Study also documented a powerful, graded effect of childhood trauma on suicide attempts throughout the lifespan (Dube et al., 2001).

1.7 Assessment Procedures

Because suicide cannot be predicted, risk assessment based on the available information is the expected standard of care

Assessing the risk of suicide is a critical responsibility for clinicians. Since suicide cannot be predicted, making an assessment of risk based on available information is the expected standard of care. Failure to assess risk is an egregious professional error by the therapist (Berman et al., 2006). Suicide risk assessment requires careful questioning while maintaining rapport with the patient. This is more challenging than is commonly understood. Patients are often not asked about suicide, even by experienced clinicians. (Bongar et al., 1998). It is important to ask about suicide in a manner that can be experienced as part of a caring conversation. Asking about suicide can sometimes be accompanied by anxiety on the part of the clinician, and lead to questioning in a rote or stiff manner, and patients can frequently sense the clinician's discomfort. Clinician's must be sufficiently comfortable with doing suicide risk assessments that they can ask the necessary questions to get the information they need to estimate risk. Ideally, patients will experience this as a deepening of the therapeutic conversation, rather than as a detour or distraction from what they feel they really need to talk about.

There is no one standard way to ask the question about suicide, nor one standard time in a session when the question should be asked. What is important is that the question be clear, direct, and specific. Terms like "hurting yourself" or "harming yourself" could be misconstrued. At times, suicide can be asked about as part of a two-step inquiry. For example, asking first about hopelessness and then about suicide, or first about the wish to be dead and then about suicide. However, even if hopelessness or the wish to be dead are denied, the question about suicide should still be asked.

Clinical Pearl
Examples of Questions About Suicide

- Are you thinking about suicide?
- Are you thinking about killing yourself?
- Are you thinking about ending your life?
- Do you ever feel hopeless? Have you ever felt so hopeless that you wanted to kill yourself?
- Do you ever wish you were dead? When you have wished you were dead, did you ever think of suicide?

The simple denial of suicidal ideation is insufficient evidence to determine an absence of suicide risk. One study of 76 suicides that occurred during inpatient hospitalization or immediately after discharge reported that 78% of the patients had denied suicidal ideation when last assessed (Busch et al., 2003).

While some of these denials may have been truthful, many patients may have concealed their suicidal thoughts; either because they were already planning their death and did not want to be stopped, or because they did not want to be forced to remain in the hospital. This underscores the importance of mastering the art of eliciting information about suicidal ideation. Emphasizing that talking about suicidal thoughts with your therapist does not mean automatic, involuntary hospitalization is extremely important and can help provide a greater sense of safety and control for the patient. An example is given in Clinical Vignette 4.

Clinical Vignette 4
Probing for Suicidal Ideation

Bob was attending his first outpatient appointment after being discharged from an inpatient psychiatric unit following a suicide attempt. His therapist asked him if he had any suicidal thoughts since he was discharged 4 days previously. Bob, hesitated for a moment, and then said "no." His therapist, noticing the hesitation told Bob that continuing to have suicidal thoughts did not mean he would be forced back into the hospital. The therapist explained that he frequently treated people with suicidal thoughts in outpatient therapy, and that therapy was most likely to be helpful if he could talk openly about his suicidal thoughts and what led him to have those thoughts. The therapist further explained that he would only intervene against Bob's wishes if he was convinced that Bob was planning on killing himself within the next several days and was unwilling to work to keep himself safe. Bob then acknowledged that he had thought about suicide 2 days ago when his daughter had yelled at him after he had punished her for coming in after curfew. The suicidal thoughts were transient and had not recurred since the argument. Further, Bob's rifle had been taken out of the home by his brother during the inpatient hospitalization. Bob stated," With the gun gone, I don't even know how I would kill myself." They explored what made the interaction with his daughter so painful that he had thoughts about suicide and at the end of the session they invited Bob's wife into the session and discussed that it was likely that Bob would have some suicidal thoughts from time to time. The therapist encouraged Bob both to let his wife know if he was having these thoughts as well as to contact the therapist and gave both of them instructions about how to contact the therapist after hours, as well as the number for the local psychiatric emergency service.

Because of potential reluctance to disclose suicidal thoughts, it is important for clinicians to be attuned to nonverbal cues when talking about suicide. A delayed response, reluctance to make eye contact, a sigh or a moment's agitation could all be signs that suicidal thoughts are present. Additional promising techniques for eliciting suicidal ideation have been developed by Shea (2002), who describes the importance of *validity techniques* – approaches to interviewing that can be used to ask about a variety of issues that are often concealed, such as substance abuse or domestic violence, as well as for inquiries about suicide.

Clinicians should be attuned to nonverbal cues when talking about suicide with patients

Examples of these techniques include the behavioral incident where questions are focused on obtaining descriptions of behavior rather than obtaining opinions, for example, "What did you drink yesterday?" rather than "Do you have a drinking problem?" Likewise, "Just before you took the 12 aspirin, what thoughts were going through your mind?" is superior to "When you took the pills, do you think you were really trying to kill yourself?" Other examples of validity techniques include *shame attenuation, gentle assumption*, and *normalization*. An example of normalization would be, "People who feel depressed and hopeless frequently think about suicide. Have you ever had thoughts about ending your life?"

Once a patient has acknowledged suicidal ideation, it is very important to get additional information about the person's suicidal thoughts. Suicidal thoughts can vary in frequency and in intensity. They may be experienced as intrusive and difficult to ignore or transitory and easier to dismiss. It is also important to understand what has led to the thoughts and the consequences of having these thoughts. Suicidal thoughts may be triggered by certain contexts, such as an argument with someone, and for many persons with chronic suicidal ideation, their suicidal thoughts function as escape behavior, an automatic response to intense emotional pain. It is especially important to remember that suicidal thoughts are typically connected to the patient's deepest pain. By attempting to understand a patient's suicidal thoughts we are simultaneously trying to understand what most distresses them, what they experience as most intolerable, and why. Ultimately, a suicide risk assessment should be part of a caring conversation in which the therapist is practiced enough in assessing risk that the patient should experience no discordance between their telling of their story and the therapist's assessment of risk.

Clinical Pearl
Additional Questions About Suicide

- How often do you think of killing yourself?
- When did the suicidal thoughts start?
- How long do the thoughts last?
- How intense are the thoughts?
- Did you tell anyone about the thoughts? How did they respond?
- When were your suicidal thoughts the most intense?
- After you started to think about suicide, did you do anything to act on the thoughts?
- Did you think about how you would kill yourself?
- Do you have a firearm available to you?
- Have you thought about where you would kill yourself?
- Have you ever made a suicide attempt?
- Have you ever taken any actions in preparation for making a suicide attempt?
- (If the patient reports they have not made a suicide attempt) What is the closest you have come to acting on your suicidal thoughts?

There is a long history in suicidology of searching for reliable and valid suicide assessment instruments that can inform the clinical assessment of suicide risk (Rogers & Oney, 2005). Prediction of death by suicide was probably never a feasible goal, so attention has turned instead to assessment of risk, rather than prediction.

Range and Knott (1997) published a review of 20 suicide assessment instruments, including scales that relied upon clinician rating, self- rating, those assessing buffers against suicide, measures for adolescents and children, and more specialized instruments. Based on their review of the existing reliability and validity data, and their ease of administration in clinical settings, they recommended the Beck Scale for Suicidal Ideation (Beck et al., 1979), the Reasons for Living Inventory (Linehan et al., 1983), and the four-item version of Linehan's (1981) Suicidal Behaviors Questionnaire.

Despite these extensive efforts, early survey information regarding how clinicians actually assess risk in real world settings found that clinicians rarely used suicide specific risk assessment tools (Jobes et al., 1995). In attempting to understand the reasons for this, Jobes (2006) concluded that clinicians tended to pervasively rely on the clinical interview and perceived suicide risk assessment tools as impractical and without clear treatment or management implications. There was also a perception that such instrument failed to capture essential but elusive aspects of suicidality (Jobes, 2006). That reluctance to use specific suicide risk assessment tools may now be changing with the more widespread use of the Patient Health Questionnaire 9 (PHQ-9) and the Columbia Suicide Severity Rating Scale (CSSRS).

Clinical use of such instruments must always be as a component of a more thorough suicide risk assessment utilizing a clinical interview. However, the combination of interview and assessment instruments does have much to recommend it. By utilizing both, consistency between responses can be explored. The relationship context is very important to understand with regard to the use of assessment instruments. For some, suicidality may be more likely to be disclosed on self-report forms than in an interview, particularly when the interviewer is a stranger. There may be a particular utility in combining interview and assessment instruments upon intake or initial interview, when there is not yet an existing, collaborative relationship. The use of an instrument that focuses on the client's wish to die, combined with an instrument like Linehan's questionnaire that focuses on reasons for living, may be particularly important, as only by doing so can we fully appreciate the client's ambivalence about suicide, assessing both the wish to die and the desire to live.

Rogers and Oney (2005) emphasize the importance of the relationship context in suicide risk assessment.

Clinician's may respond to concerns about suicide by becoming preoccupied with assessing risk, and this can lead to not paying sufficient attention to the therapeutic relationship. Being asked endless questions about suicidality can lead to a disconnection with patients, especially if they feel there is no engagement with their pain but rather a focus on the therapist's own anxiety and concerns about liability. Supplementing the interview with assessment instruments can thus help meet the therapist's need for additional information without overwhelming patients with too many questions that are disconnected from the pain driving them toward suicide or the buffers keeping them alive.

Combining clinical interview with assessment instruments is recommended

Rogers and Oney (2005) point out that the Suicide Status Form devised by Jobes as part of the Collaborative Assessment and Management of Suicidality (CAMS; Jobes, 2006) includes an explicit focus on collaborative assessment. The Suicide Status Form is part of an overall process of clinical assessment, treatment planning, and management of suicidal risk for suicidal outpatients that has collaboration at its core. The Suicide Status Form is used within the CAMS approach to conduct an initial, multidimensional assessment of suicide risk, develop a suicide-specific treatment plan, track and document ongoing suicidal risk, and determine and document clinical outcomes. Jobes' system is an example of the important connections between initial risk assessment, treatment planning, ongoing monitoring of suicidal risk, and documentation of outcomes.

In recent years, the use of suicide risk assessment tools has expanded significantly, driven by research on large numbers of administrations of tools such as the PHQ-9 and the CSSRS (Posner et al., 2007). The large-scale adoption of such instruments, which is now underway, has the potential for reducing the problematic variability in how suicidal ideation is assessed and responded to in diverse clinical settings.

Responses to question 9 of the PHQ-9 were found to be a strong predictor of suicide attempts and a moderate predictor of suicide attempts

The PHQ-9 was used in a study conducted with patients being seen for depression by primary care and mental healthcare providers at Group Health Cooperative. The study examined answers to question 9 which asks, "Over the last two weeks, how often have you been bothered by thoughts that you would be better off dead, or of hurting yourself in some way?" with response options of *not at all*, *several days*, *more than half the days*, or *nearly every day*. There were over 200,000 administrations to over 40,000 patients. Responses to question 9 were found to be a strong predictor of suicide attempts and a moderate predictor of suicide death (Simon et al., 2016). The PHQ-9 is now used frequently as a depression screen in settings all across the country and in fact around the world allowing for big data analytics to be conducted. In a study of patients who answered *not at all* to question 9, but who later made a suicide attempt, two types of explanations emerged. One group reported that at the time of the screening they had not been thinking about suicide. The other group reported that they had concealed their suicidal ideation out of concern about being forced into a hospital or otherwise losing control. It should be noted that the fact that there was a subgroup who concealed their suicidal thinking is not a reason to not ask the question as many with suicidal thinking did reveal it and these people were able to receive treatment they otherwise might not have received.

Another instrument now in large scale use is the CSSRS. This instrument asks detailed questions about suicidal ideation and behavior and its differentiation of preparatory behavior and aborted and interrupted suicide attempts has been a significant step forward in suicide risk assessment. Since planning for suicide and taking any kind of preparatory action have been shown to be more associated with suicidal behavior than the presence of suicidal ideation alone, this type of assessment allows for a more informed triaging and risk stratification. The CSSRS, by allowing for a finer differentiation of risk, is often used as a second level assessment instrument if someone has a positive response to question 9 on the PHQ-9. By reducing so called false positives, intensive treatment resources can be used more appropriately. For youth, the Ask Suicide Screening Questions (ASQ) was developed by the National Institute of Mental Health and is a set of four screening questions that identified 97% of youth ages 10–21 years who were at risk for suicide (Horowitz et al., 2012). Also King and colleagues (2021) developed and validated the Computerized Adaptive Screen for Suicidal Youth (CASSY) to predict a suicide attempt within 3 months. With this tool, as youth move through the screening, questions adapt to the user's previous answers to measure different pathways to risk.

2

Theories and Models of Suicidal Behavior

2.1 Neuropsychiatric Theories

In the United States over 90% of deaths by suicide are associated with diagnosable mental disorder

Neuropsychiatric theories of suicide emphasize the genetic and biomedical vulnerabilities associated with these tragic deaths. An important method for estimating the contribution of genetics to suicide are twin studies, which compare the concordance of death by suicide among identical twins who share the same genetic material, to fraternal twins who do not. In a review of twin studies of deaths by suicide, Roy and colleagues (1997) found that out of 129 identical twin pairs, there were 17 occasions when both twins died by suicide. In contrast, out of 270 nonidentical twin pairs, there were only two times when both twins died by suicide. This difference provides strong evidence for the important contribution of genetics to suicide.

Additional evidence comes from adoption studies in which the rate of suicide among biological relatives of adoptees was found to be higher than among the adopted families (Shulsinger et al., 1979). However, as Jamison (1999) points out, the concordance rate of 15%, while supporting a genetic contribution, also demonstrates that psychological and environmental factors have a clear role. In fact, the concordance rate for suicide is actually less than for severe mental illnesses such as manic depression and schizophrenia (Jamison, 1999).

The genetic contribution to suicide presumably acts by creating a biological vulnerability, which then interacts with environmental factors to intensify risk. A frequently replicated finding is the association between suicide risk and low levels of CSF 5-HIAAA, a metabolite of serotonin (Jamison, 1999). Persons with mood disorders who attempted suicide and who had low levels of this serotonin metabolite were more likely to die by suicide within a year than those with higher levels (Asberg, 1997). Postmortem studies have also found serotonin abnormalities in the prefrontal cortex of the brain (Stanley & Stanley, 1989), which could be associated with disinhibition or impulsivity. The potential role of the serotonin system in suicidal behavior is important for two other reasons: Early adverse events have been shown to impact the serotonergic system and with the widespread use of selective serotonin reuptake inhibitors (SSRIs), there was hope that these medications could reduce suicide (Institute of Medicine et al., 2002). While these medications are demonstrably effective as treatments for depression, their effectiveness in preventing suicide is still uncertain. In addition, there has been concern that prescribing SSRIs to youth could increase suicidal ideation or attempts for some (Friedman, 2014).

The stress–diathesis model of suicidal behavior proposes that stressful events can be precipitants for suicide in individuals with a diathesis or underlying biological vulnerability (Mann & Currier, 2010). Research has focused on investigating the main systems involved with stress response, the noradrenergic system, and the hypothalamic–pituitary–adrenal axis to identify abnormalities.

Additional neuropsychiatric research has focused on neuroimaging studies of those who have attempted suicide. These studies have utilized a variety of neuroimaging techniques such as magnetic resonance imaging (MRI), positron emission tomography (PET), diffusion tensor imaging (DTI), and single photon emission computed tomography (SPECT). These studies found significant structural and functional deficits in several areas of the suicidal brain (Sudol & Oquendo, 2016).

Most mental health professionals believe suicide results from complications of untreated mental disorders, and that suicide reflects the severity of those disorders. For example, a person with untreated major depression that does not remit may eventually become hopeless and suicidal. Indeed, psychological autopsy studies, which use multiple informants to delve deeply into the lives of those who have died by suicide, have consistently shown that in the United States over 90% of suicide deaths are associated with diagnosable mental disorder (Institute of Medicine et al., 2002).

However, while acknowledging the link between mental illness and suicide, the IOM, in its landmark summary of the field entitled *Reducing Suicide: A National Imperative,* emphasized that in some cultures, such as China, there is not a prominent link between mental illness and suicide (Institute of Medicine et al., 2002). In addition, the fact that the majority of those with the types of mental illness most associated with suicide, such as depression or substance abuse, do not die by suicide underscores the complex biopsychosocial nature of suicide and makes it difficult to conceptualize suicide as solely a complication of mental disorders or as a behavior that simply reflects an exacerbation of a mental disorder. Best estimates are that suicide rates among those who had previously been treated for a depressive disorder as inpatients are about twice as high (4.1%) as the rates for those who had been treated as outpatients (2%). Those treated as inpatients following suicide ideation or suicide attempts are about 3 times as likely to die by suicide (6%) as those who were only treated as outpatients (Bostwick & Pancratz, 2000). Yet even among this high-risk group, the vast majority do not die by suicide.

2.2 Psychological Theories

The question of why people kill themselves has been asked for millennia, but psychological science has only been meaningfully brought to bear on this critical question over the last half-century.

Several psychological theories have made important contributions to our understanding of suicide. While the link between mental illness and suicide is clear, the majority of those with depression or substance abuse as risk factors do not die by suicide. While comorbidity further increases the risk, this is still not a sufficient explanation for why the majority of those with these two potent risk factors do not die by suicide.

The first major psychological theory was developed by Edwin Shneidman, the father of suicide prevention in the United States. Shneidman posited that suicidal behavior had a purpose, and that it is an attempt to escape from unendurable psychological pain. He called this psychological pain *psychache* (Shneidman, 1996). Without this deep psychological pain, there is no suicide. He also described the role of *perturbation*, a concept similar to agitation or emotional volatility. Research on the role of anxiety as an acute risk factor for suicide appears to support this concept (Busch et al., 2003). Shneidman also was the first to speak systematically about lethality. As Joiner (2005) points out, not all those with overwhelming psychological pain will engage in lethal self-destructiveness.

Shneidman proposed ten commonalities of suicide (see Box 3). For, example he proposed that cognitive constriction was a common characteristic of the suicidal individual. Suicidal people have "tunnel vision" and do not see alternatives to suicide as solutions for ending their pain. He also believed the most common emotions in suicide were hopelessness and helplessness.

Ambivalence about suicide can continue right up until the moment of death

Shneidman was the first person to emphasize that suicidal individuals are typically ambivalent about dying. This ambivalence can continue right up until the moment of death. Anecdotes from some who have survived jumping off the Golden Gate Bridge describe how moments after jumping these individuals regretted their action. Similarly, it is not uncommon in clinical practice to encounter individuals who have called a hotline or ambulance after taking an overdose. This is at times misinterpreted as meaning the suicide attempt was not serious. However, this behavior is best interpreted as a manifestation of the ambivalence that is so common among suicidal persons.

Building on the foundation of psychological theory laid down by Shneidman, other theorists have made additional important contributions. For example, cognitive behavioral theories have made major contributions to the understanding of suicide. Two salient examples include Aaron Beck and Marsha Linehan. Beck emphasized the significant role of hopelessness as a risk factor. He provided the research that confirmed Shneidman's initial observations. In a study of 207 patients hospitalized for suicidal ideation, only hopelessness predicted the 14 who died by suicide over the next decade (Beck et al., 1985). Beck also posited the role of cognitive sensitization. Over time, with repetition, suicide-related thoughts or behaviors become favored (Beck, 1996). Additional research has explored other significant cognitive variables first identified by Shneidman that may constitute core components of suicidality. What makes a person view their situation as unendurable? What drives the compulsion to act? And what determines the sense that there are no other options than suicide? One important line of research has focused on *overgeneral memory*, a form of autobiographical memory that focuses on a person's life history (Williams et al., 2006). Suicidal persons tend to not remember events in their personal history in specific detail. Instead, these events are recalled generally and the memories are colored by the person's depression and hopelessness.

Box 3
Shneidman's 10 Commonalities of Suicide

- The common purpose of suicide is to seek a solution.
- The common goal of suicide is cessation of consciousness.
- The common stimulus for suicide is unbearable psychological pain. The common stressor in suicide is frustrated psychological needs. The common emotion in suicide is hopelessness-helplessness.
- The common cognitive state in suicide is ambivalence. The common perceptual state in suicide is constriction.
- The common action in suicide is escape.
- The common interpersonal act in suicide is communication of intention. The common pattern in suicide is consistency of lifelong styles.

Reprinted by permission of Oxford Publishing Limited, Inc. from Shneidman, E. S. (1996). *The suicidal mind.* Oxford University Press.

Williams also points out that different general pathways may exist for suicidal behavior. One pathway is believed to be driven by hopelessness while the other is strongly related to failures in affect regulation. In hopelessness driven suicide, a sense of entrapment would escalate to suicidality through repeated failures in solving problems and resulting hopelessness. Affect driven suicidal behavior may result from a fundamental failure of affect regulation and the intrusion of distressing memories.

Chronically suicidal persons frequently experience intense emotions in response to a wide variety of cues

Linehan (1993) has developed the most significant scientific analysis of the role of emotion in suicidal behavior. Her theory and treatment for chronically suicidal women grew out of her experiences with clients who met the diagnostic criteria for borderline personality disorder. Using the most recent understandings of the science of emotion and embedding her work within a functional analytic perspective, she has added a powerful, new dimension to empirically informed treatments for suicidal behavior. Emotional dysregulation is a key concept in Linehan's model. Chronically suicidal persons frequently experience strong emotions; they respond emotionally to a wide variety of cues and their responses are intense. They have difficulty tolerating this emotional distress without resorting to behaviors that help them escape or moderate these intense and painful emotions. Linehan also describes the complex behavioral chains that often exist, including emotions triggering other emotions, such as anger triggering guilt or shame triggering anxiety. Her approach has also focused on suicidal behavior and its functions. Suicidal behavior can be either operant or respondent; it can be reinforced by its consequences or it can be a direct response to a stimulus. Suicidal behavior will frequently function as escape behavior, as noted by Shneidman. Not only is the ultimate aim of suicidal behavior frequently an escape from emotional pain, but the very act of self-harm and self-injury can function as an escape from emotional pain, insofar as the attention of the person making the attempt becomes focused on the attempt itself rather than the emotional pain the person is experiencing. Indeed, even suicidal ideation can be negatively reinforced, as the very thought of suicide can function as an escape (albeit only momentary) from pain.

While Linehan has focused on the development of suicidal behavior generally, Joiner (2005) has focused on what produces lethal suicidal behavior. Joiner has emphasized that human beings do not easily come to an act of final, lethal self-destruction. For most of us, the fear of death is stronger than any other motivation. Our determination to survive has been developed over hundreds of thousands of years of human evolution. What leads this incredibly powerful behavioral tendency in people to not only be overcome but reversed, so that a person becomes the deliberate agent of their own death? Joiner emphasizes that, for this to occur, a capacity to enact lethal self-injury must be learned. Individuals are not born with this capacity for lethal self- injury, and people who die by suicide have to work their way up to it. They must lose their natural fear of death and pain in order to undertake an extreme and difficult form of action. How is this fear reduced? According to Joiner (2005), this occurs through a form of practice involving repeated desensitizing exposure. The most obvious form of such practice is found in suicide attempts, the greatest single predictor of death by suicide.

With repeated exposure there is habituation. Not only are cultural or personal taboos against suicide eroded, but the fear of death and the pain associated with suicide attempts gradually diminishes. One can see in many patients an escalating pattern of increased lethality of suicide attempts (Beautrais, 2004), leading to ultimate death by suicide. In this model, suicidal ideation can also be seen as a form of habituation, as repeated imaginal exposure to the idea of suicide reduces the fear. Joiner theorizes that opponent processes may play a role.

One can see in some patients an escalating pattern of increased lethality of suicide attempts

Opponent process theory predicts that with repetition, the effects of a provocative stimulus diminish, and the opposite effect, or opponent process, becomes amplified and strengthened.

Joiner (2005) emphasizes that both suicidal desire and suicidal capacity must be present before a suicide occurs. People who die by suicide must both want to kill themselves and be able to kill themselves. Joiner argues that there are those who want to die by suicide but cannot, as well as those who can but do not want to (Joiner, 2005). While the concept of lethality has long been an important component of theoretical and clinical work with suicidal people, Joiner's unique contribution has been the recognition that people must acquire the capacity to enact lethal self-injury. The natural and profound inhibitions humans possess against suicide are only overcome through repeated, desensitizing experiences. This desensitizing can take place through suicide attempts, suicidal ideation, witnessing violence and trauma, or other provocative experiences. These are the people who kill themselves, according to Joiner (2005) (see summary in Box 4).

The capacity to enact lethal self-injury is acquired

Joiner has also emphasized the role of perceived burdensomeness and failed belongingness as suicide risk factors. He views these as critical in determining why a person wants to die by suicide. Building on Shneidman's notion that psychache, or unendurable psychological pain, is central to suicide, Joiner (2005) argues that those who want to die by suicide are often those who perceive themselves as a burden on others or who do not perceive themselves as belonging. Many suicidal people no longer regard themselves as effective members of their families or communities, but instead regard themselves as burdens. It is this experience of self as a burden to those one loves that may play a critical role in dying by suicide despite the presence of supportive, caring others. When encountered in psychotherapy, this maladaptive belief system must be vigorously addressed. Failed belonging is related to the painful experience of social isolation.

Box 4
Summary of Joiner's Theory on Suicide (2005)

To die by suicide people must want to kill themselves and be able to kill themselves.
Who wants to die by suicide?
Those who feel that they are a burden upon others or feel they do not belong.
Who is able to die by suicide?
Those who have acquired the capacity for lethal self-injury.

Other theorists have endeavored to build on the foundation of Joiner's groundbreaking work, including the notion that what drives the development of suicidal ideation is different than what propels an individual to act on their suicidal thoughts. O'Connor's integrated motivational–volitional model (2011) posits that feelings of defeat and entrapment are the critical drivers of becoming suicidal while acquired capacity along with other factors, such as impulsivity and access to lethal means, determine whether suicidal thoughts are acted upon. Klonsky and May (2015) have proposed what they call the three step theory (3ST) which is also based on the hypothesis that the processes responsible for the development of suicidal ideation are different than those that are responsible for suicidal ideation progressing to suicidal behavior. They regard pain and hopelessness as the primary drivers of suicidal ideation with both needing to be present for a person to become suicidal. They also hypothesize that connectedness is a key protective factor against escalating suicidal ideation. Disrupted connectedness through factors such as thwarted belongingness and perceived burdensomeness diminishes such protection. Finally, they take the construct of capacity for suicide and divide it into dispositional, acquired, and practical contributors to the capacity to attempt suicide (Klonsky & May, 2015). Dispositional refers to biological or genetic contributors to suicide capacity mediated through variables such as pain sensitivity.

Acquired capacity is mainly the concept described by Joiner (2005) in which habituation to experiences associated with pain, injury, fear, and death occurs. Practical contributors refers to variables such as knowledge of and access to lethal means facilitating a suicide attempt. An additional recent elaboration is the application of the cusp catastrophe model to the emergence of suicidal behavior. Bryan and colleagues (2019) found by monitoring suicidal ideation among psychiatric outpatients that large sudden shifts in baseline suicidal ideation signaled the later emergence of suicidal behavior.

Clinical Pearl
Acquiring the Capacity for Lethal Self-Injury

For years, I have heard from many patients who were having suicidal thoughts that they did not believe they had the "courage" to kill themselves. I listened to these statements without quite understanding what I was hearing. Because I did not believe suicide was an act of "courage," having spoken to too many families grievously wounded by a death by suicide, I did not pay sufficient attention to these statements. These patients were telling me they had not yet acquired the capacity for lethal self-injury, although that did not mean they would not acquire this capacity in the future.

3

Risk Assessment and Treatment Planning

Treatment for individuals at risk for suicide must begin with a treatment plan based on a comprehensive suicide risk assessment. This presumes that suicidality was either the reason for treatment or was uncovered during the initial assessment. When suicidality emerges during the course of treatment (i.e., a person with no past history of suicidal behavior makes a suicide attempt or discloses suicidal ideation while in treatment), the treatment plan should be immediately modified to address the suicide risk. This does not mean that other issues previously being addressed in therapy need to be dropped, but neither should there be a return to treatment as usual.

Treatment planning for individuals at risk for suicide should always directly target the individual's suicide risk, and include attention to how suicide risk will be assessed, managed, and treated on an ongoing basis.

Treatment planning for people at risk for suicide should always directly target the individual's suicide risk

Berman and colleagues (2006) have emphasized that too often clinicians utilize the treatment they are comfortable with rather than directly addressing suicidal behavior.

Not directly addressing suicidal behavior in the treatment plan is often associated with the view that treating the underlying diagnostic conditions is synonymous with addressing suicidal risk. The clear link between mental illness and suicide has led mental health professionals to assume that by treating the underlying disorder (e.g., depression or substance abuse), suicide risk can be reduced and suicide prevented. However, there is little evidence this is the case (Linehan, 2008). The systematic exclusion of suicidal patients from both medication and psychotherapy trials mean that the efficacy for reducing suicide risk of many treatments for the diagnostic conditions associated with suicide are simply unknown. The implications of this lack of evidence is certainly not that such disorders should go untreated, nor that treating the underlying disorder should not be part of the treatment plan. There is compelling logic for using treatment to modify any risk factors whenever possible. For example, reducing substance abuse clearly is an important goal in the treatment of suicidal persons. The problem is assuming that treating the underlying disorder is sufficient to prevent suicide. It is not, and it is important for therapists to treat the suicidal behavior, thoughts, or desires directly. Treating suicidality directly is the common thread among the growing list of therapies that have now been shown to reduce suicidal behavior.

Not including suicide risk in the treatment plan makes the clinician seem oblivious to the possibility of suicide or a suicide attempt

This direct attention on suicide risk must be reflected in the treatment plan as well. Not including suicide risk in the treatment plan makes the clinician seem oblivious to the possibility of suicide or suicide attempts. For patients with a past history of suicidal thoughts or behavior, the possibility must be anticipated.

Clinical Pearl
Treatment Planning With Suicidal Persons

- Identify the pain driving the suicidal thoughts or behavior
- Assess risk and protective factors
- Estimate risk level from risk and protective factor information
- Distinguish between acute and chronic risk levels
- Resolve contradictory risk factors
- Determine whether risk and protective factors can be modified
- Target interventions to lower risk factors or increase protective factors

Every comprehensive clinical assessment needs to answer several key questions. These include determining the current level of suicide risk (including whether an acute emergency exists that requires emergency intervention) and obtaining information about risk and protective factors that may need to be addressed in long- term treatment planning. This must be accomplished while maintaining a flexible and collaborative relationship with the patient that allows them to tell their story and explain the pain that is leading them to consider ending their life.

3.1 Assessing Suicide Risk and Protective Factors

The treatment plan should identify both risk and protective factors, estimate risk based on these factors (including how risk may be expected to change over time), determine whether risk and protective factors can be modified, and explain how the treatment plan will attempt to reduce this risk level.

Assessing suicide risk factors should include, but not be limited to, examining the roles of depression and substance abuse. As Joiner suggests, those who die by suicide will be those who have the desire to, and who have also acquired the capacity to do so. Suicidal ideation is very prevalent among those with major depressive episodes with almost 30% of them having seriously considered suicide, indicating an intense desire to die (Piscopo et al., 2016). Those who abuse substances may be more likely to experience the kind of provocative experiences that will increase the capacity to inflict lethal self-harm.

But in addition to depression and substance abuse, other risk factors must be assessed as well (see Box 5).

Social withdrawal, social isolation, and the experience of oneself as a burden to loved ones must be explored. The patient's sense of belonging and the existence of meaningful social connections should be actively assessed and addressed in the treatment plan. Social withdrawal is common in depression, and substance abuse can cause alienating conflict. It is noteworthy that the research of Murphy and colleagues (1979) on suicide in alcoholics identified interpersonal conflict as a major precipitant. However, neither depression nor substance abuse needs to be present for these risk factors to contribute to increased risk.

Additional risk factors to be assessed include the presence of past suicidal behavior, access to potentially lethal means, including firearms, as well as hopelessness and impulsivity.

Assessing for protective factors is a critical but sometimes neglected part of the suicide risk assessment as well. At times, the protective factors can be the mirror image of the risk factors. For example, social isolation is a risk factor while social connection a protective factor. A history of reaching out for help when in a suicidal crisis is a protective factor; a history of not reaching out for help when in a suicidal crisis is a risk factor. Various cultural and religious beliefs may serve to inhibit acting on suicidal thoughts. However, assumptions cannot be made on the basis of nominal religious affiliations. There must be a discussion in order to learn how a person's spiritual life impacts their suicide risk.

Box 5
Risk Factors for Suicide

- Mental disorders, particularly mood disorders, schizophrenia, anxiety disorders, eating disorders, and borderline personality disorder
- Alcohol and other substance use disorders
- Hopelessness
- Impulsiveness and/or aggression
- Trauma and abuse
- Previous suicide attempt (efforts to prevent discovery and regret upon survival convey additional risk)
- Relational or job loss
- Access to lethal means
- Social isolation
- Perceived burdensomeness
- Difficulty asking for help
- Barriers to accessing healthcare, particularly behavioral healthcare
- Insomnia

3.2 Estimating Suicide Risk Level

Estimating the level of suicide risk from the risk and protective factor information obtained during the assessment is a complex process. It is useful to combine the initial interview with self-report instruments, such as the PHQ-9, the Beck Scales, or the CSSRS. Linehan's (1983) Reasons for Living Inventory is particularly valuable for assessing protective factors. However, there is no psychometric formula that can tell the clinician precisely how to estimate the level of risk. In fact, some question whether suicide risk assessment that puts people in risk categories of high, moderate, or low should be done at all (Murray, 2016). They argue that these risk categories are poorly defined and without valid empirical anchors and lead to an overreliance on hospitalization. Rather than making clinical decisions on the basis of low, moderate, and high-risk categories they argue that all those at elevated risk should receive evidence-based care. While there is certainly merit in the argument that all those at risk should receive good care, doing away with risk categories would be problematic in several different ways. It is clear that the intensity of suicide risk does vary between individuals in a way that has dramatically different implications for clinical intervention. The person who has held a loaded gun in his hand while

There is no psychometric formula that can tell the clinician precisely how to estimate the level of risk

ruminating about suicide or who wakes up alive after taking a significant overdose is very different than the person who has had suicidal thoughts without intent or plan and has never acted on those thoughts. Assessment instruments such as the CSSRS utilize such differences to make meaningful clinical differentiations. Further, recent research in the US Department of Defense and the US Department of Veterans Affairs has been able to form very meaningful risk categories. While these advancements do not allow for short-term risk prediction, they do allow longer-term risk classification. Army STARRS was one of the largest suicide research studies ever undertaken focusing on suicide among service members in the US Army. Using sophisticated predictive analytics, they were able to show that of soldiers hospitalized for depression the largest number of suicides in the following year after discharge occurred in the highest risk category. Building on this work Veterans Administration launched a similar predictive analytics study using variables from the electronic health record which also showed a marked clustering of suicides in the highest risk groups. Veterans Administration is now utilizing a program called REACH VET to reach out to veterans who are not currently suicidal but fall into one of these high-risk categories. However, in most treatment settings clinicians do not have access to empirically derived risk algorithms so clinicians must take the risk and protective factor information they have and estimate risk based on their own empirically informed clinical judgment This does not mean that estimating suicide risk is purely subjective. It does mean that the science has not yet evolved to a point where we can know with certainty how the empirically supported risk and protective factors combine in individual cases to determine if risk is low, moderate, or high.

Suicide risk always has a time dimension

Further, suicide risk always has a time dimension. Risk is not static, and it can fluctuate greatly over time. Risk also can be acute or chronic. High, acute risk may require hospitalization while chronic risk should typically be addressed in outpatient therapy. An understanding of suicidal behavior or a suicidal crisis in the patient's past history can help the clinician anticipate the circumstances under which acute risk might emerge. For example, if a patient has made a suicide attempt after losing a job and is currently having work-related problems, it can reasonably be anticipated that loss of the current job could lead to thoughts of suicide. According to Craig Bryan, clinicans should be looking for patterns in suicidal ideation, including accelerations in the ups and downs of suicidal ideation rather than focusing on ideation at a single point in time (Pappas, 2021).

Risk monitoring is a critical component of outpatient treatment of suicidal persons. Fluctuations in risk status may necessitate intensification of treatment. Risk must be monitored systematically for patients for whom suicide has been an issue. At minimum, risk must be assessed at critical points in treatment. According to Bongar (2002), risk should be assessed at intake as well as at transitional points in treatment.

When there is evidence of increased risk, the treatment plan must be changed to respond to this increased risk or must already include provisions regarding responding to exacerbations in suicide risk levels. During periods of increased risk, risk monitoring should take place during every clinical contact.

3.3 Resolving Contradictory Risk Factors

It is critical to understand that while there is a substantial literature on risk and protective factors, there is no perfect formula for how these factors should be put together to estimate risk for an individual person. While it is reasonable to assume that risk accumulates with each additional risk factor, or is lessened with each additional protective factor, there is no empirically derived calculus for making these critical determinations. Rather, risk and protective factors form a mosaic whose pattern must be discerned. Should each risk factor be weighed equally? That seems unlikely. A history of past near-lethal suicide attempts is more worrisome than living alone. Yet, in certain clinical circumstances, living alone may be a crucial factor. So how are these differing risk factors to be weighed in making an estimation of risk? Systematic risk estimation techniques exist that assign numerical weight to different risk factors, but clinicians have been very reluctant to use them and their value for aiding near term clinical decision-making has not been established. Even the commonly used categories of low, moderate, or high risk do not have clear empirical anchors, especially when used to estimate risk in the time frames needed by clinicians. Clinicians are frequently called upon to estimate risk in the next few hours, days, or weeks. Clinicians, therefore, must rely on clinical judgment, but on a clinical judgment deeply informed by a knowledge of empirically derived risk and protective factors. In some situations, this will be straightforward. If we receive a telephone call from a patient who is intoxicated and holding a loaded gun and is voicing suicidal intent, a randomized control trial is not necessary to inform us that this person is at high and immediate risk. Yet often the clinical picture is not nearly that clear.

There is no perfect formula for estimating the risk for an individual person

Clinicians must rely on a clinical judgement deeply informed by a knowledge of empirically derived risk and protective factors

For example, the reported absence of suicidal ideation leads us to assume decreased risk, yet a recent suicide attempt will point us in the direction of increased risk. Which outweighs the other? Consider the following cases, each of which is characterized by the absence of current suicidal ideation and the presence of a recent suicide attempt, but where the estimation of risk is very different because of the presence or absence of additional risk or protective factors.

These two examples in Clinical Vignette 5 illustrate how it is the overall patterning of risk and protective factors, rather than the presence or absence of specific risk and protective factors, that must determine our estimation of suicide risk levels. How much weight the clinician will give each risk and protective factor in assessing suicide risk is the essence of clinical judgment when dealing with suicidal patients.

Clinical Vignette 5

The Differential Weighing of Suicide Risk Factors

John is a 42-year-old Caucasian male being evaluated at the request of his wife. He denies thinking about suicide but acknowledges that last night, while intoxicated, he had to be restrained by friends from jumping off a bridge. His wife also reports that he called her on the telephone from the bar where he was drinking with his friends and expressed suicidal thoughts to her, a phone call John does not recall making. John has been drinking nightly. John is assessed to be at high risk for suicide given his alcohol abuse and recent interrupted suicide attempt. It appears highly likely that he will drink and become suicidal again within the next few days. It is recommended that he be hospitalized while efforts are made to secure placement in residential alcohol treatment.

Robert came to an initial session with his wife. They both reported that two nights ago he had made a suicide attempt by overdose of approximately 15 aspirin after an argument with his wife. She had threatened to leave him if he did not get help for "his problems," which included mishandling of money, not spending time with the children, and anger control. Following his suicide attempt, Robert agreed to come to therapy and his wife agreed to not leave him as long as he was "working on his problems." He does not report any suicidal thoughts currently. He appears to be at low risk for suicide at the present time, given the absence of suicidal ideation and the apparent stabilization in the marital relationship.

3.4 Understanding the Time Dimension of Suicide Risk

Suicide risk is not static and it fluctuates over time. Someone may be at low risk today but at very high risk in the future. See Clinical Vignette 6 for an example.

In clinical practice, we are most often concerned with the patient's current level of suicide risk. When a patient leaves our office after a weekly appointment, our most basic concern is whether they will be back next week. Yet understanding whether a patient is at imminent risk is much more art than science. Despite the fact that virtually every state incorporates imminent risk (or a similar concept) into its involuntary commitment standards, there is little scientific evidence that clinicians can predict imminent risk in a meaningful way (Simon et al., 2006). A recent meta-analysis by Large and colleagues (2016) documents that there has been little progress over the past 40 years in determining imminent risk and much of the suicide literature has focused on static risk factors that cannot be considered true warning signs for suicide. Examples include demographic variables such as age or gender that cannot be modified. Warning signs of suicide are based on research identifying acute risk of suicide over a period of months rather than a period of days or hours that clinicians must utilize to make decisions about issues such as hospitalization.

Clinical Vignette 6

Suicide Risk Fluctuates Over Time

James is a 55-year-old Irish-American male. He had experienced a series of devastatingly painful major depressive episodes. He had made a series of suicide attempts of escalating lethality. His most recent suicide attempt would have been fatal if not for his unexpectedly having been found by a case worker dropping by to check on him. James was quite clear that he would rather kill himself than endure another major depression. However, he had no present plans to kill himself. While he experienced depressed mood as part of a chronic dysthymic disorder, he could endure this. What he could not tolerate was the intensified pain of the next major depressive episode he anticipated would come in the future. Given the absence of present suicidal ideation or intent, his suicide risk at the time of assessment was low but his suicide risk in the future was extremely high. He will need to be carefully monitored as any intensification of depression could lead to escalating suicide risk requiring acute intervention.

Ultimately, clinicians are responsible for doing the best they can despite the limitations of the research literature. Undoubtedly, in many situations, a clinician's belief that a person was at imminent risk has led to intervention that was lifesaving. Both clinician's and crisis line workers may receive calls from persons who have just made a suicide attempt. Despite the ambivalence expressed by making the call at all, such patients are clearly at imminent risk and typically in need of emergency medical intervention. The person contemplating suicide sitting with a loaded gun right in front of him is clearly at imminent risk. Beyond such clear situations, what constitutes imminent risk is a clinical judgment based on in depth knowledge of suicide and of the patient. An example of the importance of the time dimension in clinical decision making is given in Clinical Vignette 6.

Maintaining awareness of the time dimension of suicide risk is critical in order to recognize the appropriate role of hospitalization. A frequent misperception that patients, their families, and even providers sometimes have is that suicide risk can be eliminated during hospitalization and that patients are discharged only when their suicide risk has been eliminated. Clinical Vignette 7 provides an example. In fact, suicide risk can be reduced during the course of a successful psychiatric hospitalization, but it can rarely be eliminated. The period following discharge from hospitalization has been shown to be a high-risk time for suicide. Data from England has documented this risk, with most suicides occurring within the first month following discharge (Appleby et al., 1999).

The time dimension of suicide risk is perhaps most clearly demonstrated by this heightened risk period that follows hospitalization. In the United States, a major study of veterans similarly showed that the period after inpatient discharge was one of heightened risk, particularly the first 60 days (Valenstein et al., 2009). In a follow-up to that study, Katz and colleagues (2019) also found heightened risk for both suicide and other causes of mortality including accidental overdose during the first 30 days post discharge and continuing through the first year. Of particular importance, the National Confidential Inquiry into Suicide and Safety in Mental Health (Appleby et al., 2019) demonstrated that suicide can be reduced during this period of heightened risk.

Suicide risk is not static; risk can fluctuate greatly over time. Both patients and families need to be educated about the time dimension of suicide risk

Clinical Vignette 7

Anticipating Exacerbation of Suicidal Risk

Ronald was a 41-year-old male hospitalized following a suicide attempt by overdose. He suffered from a major depressive episode complicated by alcohol abuse. There was substantial marital disruption. His wife, Jennifer, in a telephone call with the clinician, revealed that following her husband's discharge she planned to tell him that she had decided to divorce him. She reasoned that after his discharge he would be "doing better," and that this was the best time to tell him this difficult news. The clinician encouraged her, if she had made a final decision, to inform her husband now while he was in the hospital where there was support and protection, rather than telling him after discharge when there would likely be an escalation of suicide risk with far less opportunity for clinical intervention.

3.5 Documenting Suicidal Risk

Documentation of the suicide risk assessment and treatment plan is critical. Many times, clinicians do an excellent job of assessing risk and intervening with suicidal individuals, but their documentation does not reflect the high quality of the work they did, leaving the clinician vulnerable to legal liability in the event of a tragic outcome. Gutheil (1990) describes consultation and documentation as the twin pillars of liability prevention.

Bongar (2002) emphasizes that an essential element in risk management is the maintenance of timely, meticulous records. He also points out that every significant decision point in treatment must also include a risk–benefit analysis that describes all actions that were considered, the reasons that led the clinician to make the decision, and the reasons other alternatives were rejected.

A risk–benefit analysis assists the clinician in formulating their risk estimation

It is important to realize that documentation, while critically important for managing risk and preventing liability, is not simply paperwork done to avoid a malpractice suit. See Box 6 for guidelines for documenting risk. The risk–benefit analysis that Bongar (2002) recommends is an extremely important clinical skill for all those working with people at risk for suicide and the documentation of this risk–benefit analysis assists the clinician in clearly formulating their estimation of risk. Many times, a clinician may have a strong feeling or intuition that a patient is at low or high risk. While it is important for clinicians to respect their own intuitions, it is even more important for the clinician to understand what is influencing that intuition. Skills in risk formulation can

Box 6
Guidelines for Documenting Suicide Risk Following a Suicide Attempt or During a Suicidal Crisis

All patients who are evaluated following a suicidal attempt or during a suicidal crisis should have included as part of the documentation of that evaluation a formal assessment of suicidal risk. This should include a specific statement about the overall level of suicidal risk (low, moderate, high) as well as supporting evidence to justify the overall assessment of level of suicidal risk. Relevant factors that should be used in justifying the assessment include, but are not limited to:

- Lethality of recent attempt
- Past suicide attempt history
- Degree of suicidal intent
- Availability of means, including firearms
- Presence of a plan and degree of planning
- Regret vs. relief in response to survival
- Presence of continuing suicidal ideation, including frequency and intensity
- Availability of social/family support
- Perception of being a burden
- Family history of suicide
- Presence of active psychotic symptoms
- Presence of major depression and/or hopelessness or anhedonia
- Perturbation, anxiety, or agitation
- Alcohol/drug involvement
- Impulsivity

be sharpened by the repeated process of articulating how the varying risk and protective factors were differentially weighed, and "thinking out loud for the record" (Gutheil, 1990).

It is important to document the participation of patients, and, if possible, significant others, in the development of the treatment plan, including their understanding of the potential risks and benefits of different treatment decisions, such as whether or not to hospitalize, or to utilize different treatment options such as psychotherapy and medication. Competent patients have a right to be full partners in the decision-making process and their participation should be documented (Bongar, 2002).

Documentation is necessary both at the start of therapy during the initial treatment planning process, as well as on an ongoing basis, with particular attention needed if a suicidal crisis emerges.

Both the presence and absence of the risk factors should be included in the risk assessment. The level of risk assessed should be meaningfully related to the disposition that is arranged. Since the level of risk can fluctuate on a daily basis, suicidal patients being followed on an outpatient basis should have their level of risk revised or reaffirmed in the documentation of follow-up contacts. Finally, for these kinds of cases, obtaining psychiatric and/or supervisory consultation, and documenting this consultation, is of paramount importance.

4

Treatment

While there is substantial evidence that pharmacological treatment of disorders that are risk factors for suicide (such as depression) can be effective, pharmacological studies that have targeted suicide directly have had much more equivocal results. In part, this is because clinical trials of medication have historically excluded those at risk for suicide (as have psychotherapy studies). Evidence for the effectiveness of lithium in preventing suicide is probably stronger than for any other medication (Cipriani et al., 2005). Meltzer (1999) has examined clozapine vs. olanzapine for patients with schizophrenia or schizoaffective disorder who were at high risk for suicide and found that those receiving clozapine were less likely to attempt suicide or be hospitalized for suicide risk. More recently, two national register-based cohort studies of patients diagnosed with schizophrenia in Sweden and Finland found that clozapine was the only antipsychotic consistently associated with decreased risk of suicidal outcomes. The risk for attempted or completed suicide was 36% lower in the Finnish cohort and 34% lower in the Swedish cohort (Taipale et al., 2020).

An area of significant controversy has been the relationship between the use of selective serotonin reuptake inhibitors (SSRIs) and suicide risk. While initially the major debate within the field has focused on whether the significantly increased rates of prescription of SSRIs was responsible for a decrease in national suicide rates in various countries around the world (Safer & Zito, 2007), fears about the potential role of SSRIs in causing suicide later erupted in England and the United States. This concern about suicidality as a possible side effect from the use of SSRIs led the US Food and Drug Administration to issue a black box warning. The focus of concern was initially on youths because the evidence of efficacy for treatment of depression using SSRIs among this group was much more equivocal than the evidence among adults, making the risk–benefit ratio more problematic among youths than adults. Following this warning, prescriptions of SSRIs fell significantly. When the youth suicide rate increased in 2004, after almost a decade of decline, some argued that the decrease in use of SSRIs was to blame. While there may be a subgroup of those who take SSRIs who experience an increase in suicidality (Maris, 2007), this does not mean that they are not safe for most patients, particularly those with serious depression. Gibbons and colleagues (2007b) report that among male veterans treated with SSRIs, suicide attempts decreased. However, their effectiveness in preventing death by suicide is still uncertain.

More recently, significant attention has been given to the potential of ketamine because of early studies showing a rapid antidepressant effect including rapid remission of suicidal ideation. In a randomized trial comparing intravenous infusion of ketamine to midazolam 55% showed clinically significant remission of suicidal ideation compared to 30% (Gruenbaum et al., 2018). In 2018, the US Food and Drug Administration approved the use of an esketamine nasal spray for treatment resistant depression when used along with an oral antidepressant (US Food and Drug Administration, 2018).

A review of the literature by Rudd and colleagues (2001), which focused only on nonpharmacologic interventions, revealed only 25 randomized or controlled studies that targeted suicidality. These authors divided their review into intervention studies and treatment studies. Intervention studies were those that did not provide any kind of psychotherapy or medication treatment. These studies made changes in either procedures associated with treatment (letters, phone calls) or facilitated access to mental health services and assessed any subsequent reductions in suicide attempts. Of particular note was a study by Motto (1976) that found a reduction in death by suicide over a 2-year period of patients who refused treatment, who received nondemanding letters compared to those who did not receive such letters. However, the impact was not maintained over the full 5 years of the study.

The review by Rudd and colleagues (2001) of the intervention studies yielded the following conclusions: Intensive follow-up, case management, telephone contacts, letters or home visits may improve treatment compliance over the short-term for lower risk cases. Improved ease of access (i.e., a clearly stated crisis plan) to emergency services can potentially reduce subsequent attempts and service demand by first-time suicide attempters. Their conclusions are summarized in Box 7.

In review studies published following the 2001 summary by Rudd and colleagues, the best validated approach for reducing suicidal behavior remains dialectical behavior therapy (DBT; Linehan, 1993), which has been shown in randomized control studies to reduce suicidal behavior, as well as reduce time spent in the hospital for patients with histories of chronic suicidal behavior.

Dialectal behavior therapy (DBT) is the best validated approach for reducing suicidal behavior

Box 7
Summary of the Review by Rudd, Joiner, and Rajab (2001)

Implications for clinical practice from the treatment studies were:

- Intensive, longer term treatment following a suicide attempt is most appropriate and effective for those identified at high risk as indicated by multiple attempts, psychiatric history, and diagnostic comorbidity.
- Short-term CBT, integrating problem-solving training as a core intervention, is effective at reducing suicidal ideation, depression, and hopelessness over periods of up to 1 year. Such brief approaches do not appear effective at reducing attempts over longer time frames.
- Reducing suicide attempts requires longer term treatment modalities targeting specific skill deficits such as emotional regulation, poor distress tolerance (e.g., impulsivity), anger management, and interpersonal assertiveness, as well as other enduring problems such as interpersonal relationships and self-image disturbance (e.g., personality disturbance).
- High-risk suicidal patients can be safely and effectively treated on an outpatient basis if acute hospitalization is also available and accessible.

DBT has been shown to be effective both in controlled trials compared to treatment as usual as well as when compared to expert treatment, as demonstrated in a randomized control trial (Linehan et al., 2006). More recently, a randomized controlled trial of dialectical behavior therapy adapted for adolescents has also demonstrated DBT's effectiveness (McCauley et al., 2018) As such, it is the treatment of choice for those with a history of multiple suicide attempts, particularly those who meet diagnostic criteria for borderline personality disorder. Since DBT has been primarily studied and found effective with women who have made multiple suicide attempts, there is a pressing need to research its efficacy with men who make multiple suicide attempts.

Research has shown that short-term treatments can reduce repeat suicide attempts

Research has also shown that short-term treatments can reduce repeat suicide attempts, at least among those who have made a single suicide attempt. A recent randomized control trial by Brown and colleagues (2005) documented a reduction in suicide attempts. Utilizing a 10-session cognitive therapy intervention designed to prevent repeat suicide attempts in adults who recently attempted suicide (Brown et al., 2005), participants in the cognitive therapy group were 50% less likely to reattempt than those in the usual care group. Reductions in depression and hopelessness were also demonstrated in the cognitive therapy group, although reductions in suicidal ideation were not found.

Similarly, a randomized control trial by Slee and colleagues (2008) also found reductions in reoccurrence of suicidal behavior in a group of 15–35-year-olds, who had recently engaged in either a suicide attempt or an episode of self-harm without suicidal intent, following 12 sessions of cognitive behavior therapy combined with treatment as usual, when compared to treatment as usual alone. Positive effects on suicidal cognitions, symptoms of depression and anxiety, as well as improved problem solving were found. Among the measures of suicidal cognitions impacted were subscales related to distress tolerance and perceived burdensomeness.

More recent randomized controlled trials have demonstrated reductions in suicidal behavior as well. In a study of soldiers who either attempted suicide or had suicidal ideation and intent, soldiers who received brief cognitive behavior therapy focused on suicide risk were 60% less likely to make a suicide attempt during follow-up than soldiers who received treatment as usual (Rudd et al., 2015). Similarly, randomized controlled trials of the Collaborative Assessment and Management of Suicidality (CAMS) showed reductions in suicidal ideation in a pilot study (Comtois et al., 2011) and was also found to be equivalent to DBT in reducing suicide attempts (Andreasson et al., 2016). In another study of US soldiers, CAMS was found to reduce suicidal ideation and ED visits as compared to enhanced care as usual (Jobes et al., 2017).

In a significant European study, the Attempted Suicide Short Intervention Program (ASSIP) found an 83% reduced risk of attempting suicide during a 24-month time period compared to a control group. The treatment utilized a 3–4 session protocol with the initial session being a videotaped narrative interview in which the patient provided a detailed description of what led to their suicidal behavior. The patient and therapist then watch the video together in the second session and provide a detailed reconstruction of the transition from psychological pain to suicidal action. Warning signs and safety strategies are then developed collaboratively (Gysin-Maillart et al., 2016).

In additional demonstrations of the importance of caring contacts during care transitions, Carter and colleagues (2005) replicated Motto (1976) using postcards sent as a nondemanding follow-up. They found that among patients seen in EDs for self-poisoning, the number of self-poisoning episodes was approximately halved while the proportion of patients who engaged in self-poisoning did not decrease. This study underscores the potential value of this simple intervention, and highlights the importance of continued follow-up efforts.

A significant study conducted under the auspices of WHO in five countries found a reduction in deaths by suicide using a brief ED intervention combined with follow-up over 18 months (Fleischmann et al., 2008). This is only the second randomized controlled trial ever to show a reduction in deaths by suicide, and, like Motto (1976), involved follow-up after an acute episode of suicidality.

More recently, the combination of safety planning and telephonic follow-up has been shown to reduce suicide attempts and increase linkage to mental healthcare for veterans discharged from emergency rooms following a suicide related visit (Stanley et al., 2018). Treatment of suicidal behavior can take place in various types of settings or levels of care (i.e., inpatient, outpatient, emergency). Patients are frequently hospitalized in order to provide a secure environment in which the risk of death by suicide can be minimized, although not eliminated. According to The Joint Commission inpatient suicides are one of the most frequent critical incidents in the US healthcare system (The Joint Commission, 2008). Analyses based on both national and state samples of adolescents who have engaged in nonfatal self-harm revealed that approximately 45% of those seen in EDs were either hospitalized or transferred for specialized medical care (Vajani et al., 2007). This number appears to have increased over the following decade to 70% (Owens et al., 2017). Despite this extensive use of inpatient hospitalization, the research base for inpatient hospitalization for suicidality is surprisingly weak. There are no randomized controlled trials showing a reduction in the number of suicides due to psychiatric hospitalization. In part, this is due to the difficulties in achieving adequate sample size to demonstrate reductions in deaths by suicide that plague all suicide research, as well as the systematic exclusion of those at risk for suicide from treatment studies. There also is reluctance to do studies in which patients would be randomly assigned to hospitalization vs. a nonhospital alternative. Those few studies that examined inpatient admission vs. a control treatment condition did not demonstrate reductions in self-inflicted injury (van der Sande et al., 1997; Waterhouse & Platt, 1990). Still, inpatient hospitalization is widely and understandably considered to be an essential component of the continuum of care for suicidal individuals (APA, 2003). However, inpatient hospitalization, while essential and lifesaving for some patients at some points, should not be considered the sine qua non for the treatment of suicidal individuals. In particular, reliance on hospitalization as a single, stand-alone intervention can be problematic as suicide risk can rarely be completely eliminated based on a single hospitalization and risk clearly persists after discharge. Hospitalization is not an adequate substitute for a comprehensive continuum of care.

Beautrais (2004) states that the major clinical implications of her studies of mortality and morbidity following a suicide attempt is the need for more intensive and extensive follow-up of those making a suicide attempt. In her further analysis (Gibb, Beautrais, & Fergusson, 2005), which looked at all hospitalized suicide attempters, she and her coauthors note, "Since a high-risk group within the population of those making suicide attempts cannot be reliably identified, intervention strategies should be targeted at all individuals admitted to hospital for attempted suicide" (p. 1440). These authors further recommend that since the risk of further attempts and death is greatest in the first 2 years, support and monitoring should be concentrated during this period. However, the risk remains high 10 years after an index attempt, also indicating a need for longer term support and management.

The standard of care is risk assessment, implementation of a treatment plan, collaborative safety planning, and the use of rapid follow-up

Collaborative safety planning and the use of rapid telephonic follow-up are emerging components of a standard of care

The standard of care for treatment of suicidal persons does not mandate a specific setting for treatment, such as inpatient hospitalization, nor a specific type of treatment, such as medication or psychotherapy. Rather the standard of care is that clinicians will assess the risk for suicide and implement a treatment plan that is meaningfully linked to the level of risk assessed (Bongar, 2002). Additional emerging components of the standard of care are the utilization of collaborative safety planning and the use of rapid telephonic follow-up after care episodes (National Action Alliance for Suicide Prevention, 2018) . While some of the methods and techniques that are described in the pages to come can be utilized in a variety of treatment settings (i.e., inpatient, partial care, outpatient), the primary focus is upon their use in outpatient settings.

4.1 Methods of Treatment

4.1.1 Multiphase Models

Both Linehan (1993) and Rudd and colleagues (2001) recommend the use of multiphase models for the treatment of suicidal behavior. While they use different terminology, the concepts are quite similar. Linehan's first phase of treatment directly targets suicidal behavior. Whenever suicidal behavior exists, it must be prioritized first as suicidal behavior not only brings the risk of death, it makes a life worth living impossible. As long as suicidal behavior takes place, it must be the primary target of therapy. Similarly, for Rudd and colleagues the initial phase of treatment is symptom management, which has the goals of resolving crises, reducing suicidality, instilling hope, and reducing overall symptomology.

4.1.2 Orientation and Engagement

The start of treatment is perhaps the most important time in therapy. If persons at risk for suicide do not remain in treatment, then treatment can do nothing for them. Yet, there are multiple crucial tasks that must be performed at the start of therapy. These tasks include orienting to treatment, obtaining informed consent, performing a comprehensive suicide risk assessment, connecting with the client, helping them feel understood and able to tell their story, and working collaboratively to develop a treatment plan the client feels has the potential to meet their needs, including a safety plan to assist in enhancing immediate safety.

While not assessing for suicidal risk is one type of clinical error, substituting assessment for the basic therapeutic task of establishing a relationship is another type of error, one that may be particularly problematic for patients within the health or mental health system who may experience multiple, rote assessments before actually being able to speak to someone who will listen to them. It is not surprising that there is often poor continuity of care and early dropout from treatment if a person in crisis has reached out for help and has had to be seen in multiple settings or speak to multiple people before they can tell their story and feel connected to another human being who has the potential to help them.

These issues have been addressed by Jobes (2006), Linehan (1993), and others. Jobes emphasizes the need for an initial, collaborative treatment planning session. To reduce the interpersonal distance, he sits side by side with the client during the process. Linehan also emphasizes the need to establish a strong positive relationship. "With a highly suicidal patient, the relationship with the therapist is at times what keeps her alive when all else fails" (1993, p. 98). When a suicidal client does not engage early in treatment and drops out, it is important for the therapist to reach out and reconnect. Attempts to contact the patient should be routinely made any time a suicidal client drops out of treatment.

In addition to conducting an initial, comprehensive suicide risk assessment, performing a diagnostic assessment, and making any necessary referrals, for example, to a psychiatrist if medication is needed, is an important element of care. In addition, the therapist should have already in place a process for obtaining consultation regarding the patient's care, as consultation and documentation are typically considered the twin pillars of sound risk management when working with suicidal patients. The availability of consultation will allow the clinician to respond most effectively at critical decision-making points in treatment, such as in deciding whether or not to hospitalize a patient. The agreement of a therapist and a consulting psychiatrist or other professional with hospital-admitting privileges to maintain a patient in outpatient care may help prevent hospitalizations driven chiefly by liability concerns, as the consultation documents that outpatient care was seen by two professionals as a viable plan of care.

Clinical Pearl
Tasks to Complete at Start of Treatment

- Establish a therapeutic relationship
- Orient to treatment
- Obtain informed consent
- Perform comprehensive suicide risk assessment
- Perform a diagnostic assessment
- Develop a treatment plan
- Create a collaborative safety plan

Clinical Vignette 8
Informed Consent Regarding Emergency Intervention

Michael is a 44-year-old man with a history of multiple suicide attempts and multiple hospitalizations. At the start of treatment with a new therapist, he was encouraged to disclose any suicidal ideation. Michael clearly denied current suicidal ideation but expressed concern that if he expressed suicidal ideation in the future he would be hospitalized, possibly against his will. His therapist told him, "It is very important for our work together that you are able to let me know about your suicidal thoughts. I will not initiate involuntary hospitalization procedures simply because you are having thoughts about suicide, but only if I am convinced that you are intent on killing yourself in the immediate future and you are unable to work with me on alternative ways of keeping you safe."

It is not the presence of suicidal ideation by itself, but rather the therapist's judgement that suicide is imminent that should trigger emergency intervention if the patient is unable to collaborate in staying safe.

Orientating the patient to the treatment is an important early goal of treatment. Discussing goals and expectations, reviewing roles and responsibilities, and obtaining informed consent is sound practice for work with any patient, but it is particularly important when working with suicidal patients. For example, it can be reasonably anticipated that there could be an emergency situation in which breaching confidentiality could become necessary. Such exceptions to confidentiality and the therapist's approach to them should be discussed at the start of therapy. For an example see Clinical Vignette 8. If not, the patient may be surprised and potentially feel betrayed if a breach of confidentiality occurs unexpectedly during the course of treatment. There is little disadvantage to this type of transparency. Clarification that it is not the presence of suicidal ideation by itself, but rather the therapist's judgment that suicide is imminent that would trigger emergency interventions, can be particularly important.

Both Rudd and colleagues (2001) and Linehan (1993) emphasize the importance of this initial orientation to treatment. Rudd states, "It is difficult, if not impossible, for the patient to make a realistic commitment to treatment, without a thorough understanding of just what treatment will involve and what is expected" (p. 81). Informed consent should also routinely include a discussion regarding the potential use of both psychotherapy as well as medication along with an offer to arrange a psychopharmacology consult if indicated and desired.

Linehan (1993) incorporates having patients agree as a goal of therapy to not kill themselves during the year they are asked to participate in treatment. Linehan's approach should not be confused with a no-suicide contract. In many cases the therapist can utilize the explicit commitment to the goal at later times during the treatment.

The best suicide prevention is a life worth living

The work of Linehan (1993) and Rudd and colleagues (2001) highlights the importance of first bringing suicidal behavior under control. As long as there is acute risk, this must be the focus of treatment. This means that the clinician must be familiar with how to manage high-risk situations and must also be able to integrate this information into treatment. Yet, bringing suicidal behavior under control, while essential, is not sufficient. A patient who feels miserable and would rather be dead but is not actively suicidal is at significant risk for a resurgence of suicidal behavior. The best suicide prevention is, in Linehan's words, "a life worth living." In this section, we will first look at crisis intervention and management of acute risk and then at treatment to reduce long-term risk.

4.2 Crisis Intervention and the Management of Acute Risk

For the clinician working with patients at risk for suicide, the potential need to manage an acute crisis must be anticipated, and it is essential that the clinician obtain information about both the capabilities and the limitations of the psychiatric emergency system in the communities in which the clinician practices. This should include a clear understanding of what the clinician can provide, as well as the role and limitations of EDs, crisis lines, the police, ambulance and emergency medical technicians, and psychiatric emergency services. The availability of rapid, around the clock crisis services has been shown to be associated with decreases in suicide (While et al., 2012).

The availability of rapid, around the clock crisis services is associated with decreases in suicide

Clinical Pearl
Checklist for Being Prepared for Psychiatric Emergencies

- Determine your phone availability and emergency appointment capacity
- Understand your local psychiatric emergency response system
- Know your ED characteristics (i.e., Is there mental health capacity within the emergency room? Will they consult with you prior to disposition?)
- Determine your community's mobile outreach capacity and how to access a mobile crisis team
- Know the role, capacities, and limitations of involving the police. Are they trained in CIT (crisis intervention training) or have a similar training? Weigh the risks and advantages of involving the police
- Understand the capacities of local suicide prevention hotlines and crisis centers
- Know how to arrange for a patient at acute and high risk to be voluntarily hospitalized
- Understand involuntary commitment laws including the procedures in your jurisdiction to initiate involuntary hospitalization
- Understand your own personal limits

4.2.1 Assuring Telephone Accessibility After Hours

Treating suicidal patients requires availability outside of the psychotherapy session. A patient may experience a suicidal crisis or an intensification of suicidal thoughts or intent at any time, and the clinician must anticipate this possibility. This need for greater availability is one reason many clinicians may be reluctant to take on suicidal patients. Linehan (1993), working with chronically suicidal borderline patients, has made an important contribution by emphasizing the clinician's need to be able to provide telephone consultation outside of normally scheduled psychotherapy sessions but within the context of personal limits. No clinician can tolerate being on-call 24 hours a day, 7 days a week, on an ongoing basis. Further, different clinicians will establish different limits. But a clinician must provide suicidal patients with some

Clinicians working with suicidal patients need to provide telephone availability outside of scheduled sessions

access outside of scheduled psychotherapy sessions. A clinician unwilling to provide such accessibility should not treat suicidal patients.

Moreover, for those times when the clinician is not available, there must be alternatives. Clinicians must have made defined coverage arrangements (e.g., utilizing other members of a group practice) and must have detailed information regarding the availability and limitations of local EDs, psychiatric emergency services, and crisis centers. Further, this information should be routinely conveyed to both the patient and family members/significant others when working with a suicidal patient, so that they are clearly aware of how help can be rapidly accessed in the event of an emergency.

The telephone can be an invaluable tool in managing the suicidal outpatient (Bongar, 2002). Linehan (1993) has emphasized the importance of telephone availability by the therapist to help suicidal patients use their newfound skills (such as emotional regulation or distress tolerance) as an alternative to suicidal behavior. While there has not yet been a definitive component analysis of DBT to determine the relative role of each component of the DBT treatment package to reduce suicide behaviors, including the role of telephone consultation, it makes sense that phone work would be important. The availability of a clinician who knows the patient and can prompt and encourage them to engage in alternative behaviors rather than self-destructive behavior may play a key role in skills generalization. In addition, studies of the impact of suicide prevention hotlines have found that distress, hopelessness, and suicidal intent decreased during hotline calls, and distress and hopelessness continued to decline at 2-week follow-up. Approximately 13% of callers who agreed to the follow-up spontaneously commented that they felt the call had saved their lives (Gould et al., 2007). Additional studies of follow-up calls made by crisis center counselors to suicidal callers who had agreed to receive follow-up calls showed that a significant majority of the suicidal callers felt that the follow-up calls had helped them stay safe and not kill themselves (Gould et al., 2017). If hotline calls to a person unknown to the caller and follow-up calls can have this kind of positive impact, then calls with a trusted clinician may achieve similar or better results.

4.2.2 Suicide Prevention Hotlines

The use of crisis lines or suicide prevention hotlines is an important supplement to the clinician's own availability but does not substitute for the availability of the clinician. Patients must be given clear information about the clinician's availability as well as the availability of other members of the treatment team and instructions for when a crisis hotline or psychiatric emergency service should be called.

Information on getting help after office hours should be routinely provided to patients and their families

In 2007, The Joint Commission introduced, for the first time, a national safety goal directly related to suicide prevention (The Joint Commission, 2007). This goal focused on assessing suicide risk. Included as an implementation expectation for this goal was a requirement to provide information such as suicide prevention hotline numbers to those identified as being at risk and their families for use in crisis situations.

The availability of local hotlines and crisis centers varies in different communities, so it is important to acquire information about local resources before giving a patient a hotline number. Some hotlines do not have suicide prevention capacity. For example, in many states and communities there are excellent information and referral services that utilize the 211 number. While some of these centers are so-called blended centers that can work with suicidal individuals, others do not have this capacity. Crisis centers and their associated local hotline numbers can, and do, go out of business from time to time. Yet in the age of the Internet, these numbers can live on via the web. Crisis centers can also vary according to whether they are subject to any kind of licensing or certification. Some may be affiliated with a healthcare organization and may receive accreditation through The Joint Commission or the Commission on the Accreditation of Rehabilitation Facilities (CARF). The American Association of Suicidology (AAS) also certifies crisis centers and is the only certification that focuses solely on suicide prevention. Others may receive their accreditation through organizations such as the Alliance of Information and Referral Systems (AIRS) or Contact USA, now the International Council of Helplines. Clinicians are advised to contact their local hotline/crisis center directly to determine whether round the clock suicide prevention capacity exists, whether these organizations are certified by a recognized body, and to find out how the clinician and the center can work together constructively.

A national suicide prevention hotline number is also available, 1-800-273-TALK (8255), which is funded through SAMHSA and utilizes a national network of crisis centers called the National Suicide Prevention Lifeline. Callers who use the toll-free number 1-800-273-TALK will be connected to the closest of approximately 170 crisis centers in the United States. Crisis centers participating in the network must have appropriate licensing and certification, and must meet network standards in areas such as suicide risk assessment (Joiner et al., 2007). Lifeline crisis centers must also adhere to the network's guidelines for callers at imminent risk. The National Suicide Prevention Lifeline also provides a subnetwork of crisis centers with Spanish language capacity, as well as access to a veterans' service which can be accessed by pressing 1. Recently, the Federal Communications Commission has designated a three-digit number, 988, as a new national suicide prevention hotline number in the United States to become fully operational by July 2022 (Federal Communications Commission, 2020).

A number of other nations have similar systems. England has the number 999 as a national emergency number equivalent to the use of 911 in the United States. England also has a 111 system that can be used for mental health intervention. Australia supports its own lifeline, as does Northern Ireland. Samaritans also run crisis lines in several countries.

Information should be provided regarding national and local hotlines and crisis services

4.2.3 Emergency Appointment Capability

In addition to accessibility by telephone, there may be times when it is necessary to schedule an emergency appointment with the patient. This would be indicated in those circumstances in which a telephone contact is not sufficient to reduce risk or assist the patient in coping with suicidal thoughts. The clinician's capacity to provide such appointments will be influenced by the setting in which they work and the immediacy of the patient's need to be seen. For example, a clinician handling a crisis call at night might offer to see a patient the following morning. This requires the clinician to make an assessment, in collaboration with the patient, that the patient can maintain safety until the appointment. In some circumstances, a face-to-face assessment cannot be postponed until the next day. If this is after office hours, referral to a hospital emergency room or to a mobile outreach team may be necessary. For many clinicians, this may mean that their patient may be assessed by someone who does not know them.

When suicide risk increases, increase the frequency of clinical contact and treatment

In addition to providing an emergency appointment at a time of heightened risk, clinicians should consider increasing the frequency of appointments. Welu (1977) demonstrated a decrease in suicide attempts with intensified treatment in the period/month following a suicide attempt. Potentially, such intensification of appointment frequency may reduce or prevent suicidal behavior.

4.2.4 Use of the Emergency Department (ED)

When a patient requires ED care, there may still be significant decisions that the clinician needs to make. In some instances, the decision may be straightforward, for example, in the case of a patient who has overdosed where the response will be to call 911 to dispatch emergency medical personnel. In other instances, decision-making may not be as clear cut. For example, a patient with suicidal ideation can be offered an immediate appointment in the therapist's office to assess suicidal risk. While this may be a realistic option in the afternoon or early evening, a therapist may understandably be reluctant to offer an emergency appointment at 2:00 a.m., particularly in an isolated private practice office where no one else may be present. If the patient is directed to go to the local ED, a decision will have to be made about whether the patient can safely get to the ED, whether a family member or friend can be accessed to transport the patient, or whether an ambulance or police are required to drive the patient to the hospital. Each decision has implications, both for immediate management of suicide risk as well as for the treatment relationship. For example, if a patient is directed to go to the ED, the clinician must make a careful assessment and judgment about whether this can be done safely. For example, a patient having ideation about suicide by crashing their car would be a poor choice to drive themselves to the ED. On the other hand, in some communities it may be necessary to involve the police to arrange alternative transport. The experience of having the police or an ambulance arrive at a patient's home in the middle of the night, particularly if it is not with the patient's consent, may cause acute embarrassment and disrupt the collaboration so important to the therapeutic relationship. In some jurisdictions, police transport may require placing a patient in handcuffs, something that would be unthinkable in a cardiac or other medical emergency. In some instances, the arrival of police could even precipitate a tragic outcome. Thus, such decisions should be regarded as highly significant clinical decisions that require a careful weighing of risks and benefits, and these risks and benefits should be carefully documented.

Decisions about how to transport suicidal patients to the ED require a careful weighing of risks and benefits

It is stunning that despite the life-and-death nature of this type of decision-making, there is virtually no empirical literature to guide clinicians, and clinicians rarely receive any kind of training regarding these issues. In one of the few studies to examine this critical type of decision-making, Gould and colleagues found that Lifeline crisis workers were frequently able to de-escalate imminent risk over the phone and avoid involuntary emergency rescues (Gould et al., 2017). One of the best predictors of whether or not emergency rescue could be avoided was whether the caller was willing to collaborate in keeping themselves safe. For an example of clinical decision making regarding emergency transport, see Clinical Vignette 9.

Depending on the patient's location, the nearest ED can be reached within minutes or transport may take hours. Therapists should be aware of both the strengths and limitations of what EDs can do. While EDs are typically available around the clock, making them one of the few 24-hours-a-day services available to patients at risk for suicide in the community along with crisis hotlines, they are not available in every community, and the distance between the patient and the ED can often influence the operation of the emergency system. For example, in remote and frontier regions, access to a hospital might require air or helicopter transport while in other areas multiple EDs may exist in the same community. Furthermore, it is important to be aware of the context in which many EDs operate. The 2007 IOM report, *Hospital-Based Emergency Care: At the Breaking Point*, found that many EDs in the United States are overcrowded, that emergency care is highly fragmented, and that critical specialists are often unavailable to provide emergency care (Institute of Medicine, 2007). In the United States, emergency room boarding of mental health patients has become an increasing concern.

Mental health professionals such as psychiatrists and psychologists are sometimes unavailable in EDs. While it is possible that an ED affiliated with a teaching hospital will arrange for every suicidal patient to be seen by a psychiatric resident, in other EDs, particularly smaller community hospitals in rural areas, there may be no mental health resources at all. If a therapist has privileges at the hospital, they will typically be asked to come in and see the patient or will routinely be consulted about the disposition. If a therapist does not have privileges at the hospital, they might not be contacted at all, particularly if ED staff do not know them. A meeting with ED staff prior to a crisis to review potential collaborations is recommended for all therapists working with suicidal patients. The therapist's involvement can be of great assistance, particularly in EDs with limited mental health resources, as EDs need accurate information in order to provide a competent assessment of risk and need to have access to discharge resources. In a minority of hospitals, there will be a separate and designated psychiatric ED or service that will be in charge of the patient.

Under any circumstances, therapists can reasonably rely on several services being available in hospital EDs.

First, there will be a medical evaluation, which is of particular importance if the patient has engaged in some form of self-harming behavior. It is of vital importance that information regarding suicidal behavior that the patient has engaged in be reported to the ED personnel, ideally to the physician. For example, if a patient has contacted the therapist and reported taking an overdose, it is important that the type and amount of medication that the patient says they took be reported to the ED.Second, suicidal patients will typically receive some kind of assessment of suicide risk in the ED, but this may not always be by a mental health professional. At times it may be done by the ED nurse or physician.

Finally, every ED will arrange a disposition. However, such dispositions will often be heavily influenced by the available resources, such as inpatient psychiatric beds or outpatient mental health referrals.

Clinical Vignette 9

Making Decisions About Emergency Transport

Jack telephoned his therapist at 11:00 p.m. and told her he was having suicidal thoughts. Jack was in treatment for posttraumatic stress disorder, and he had a history of one previous suicide attempt that had led to a psychiatric hospitalization. Jack and his therapist discussed coping strategies that he could utilize to get through the night, and his therapist offered him an appointment for the morning. However, after discussing Jack's ability to keep himself safe overnight with the patient and his wife, a conversation in which Jack expressed concern about his ability to not act on suicidal impulses, they agreed that he needed to be seen as soon as possible in the emergency room. They discussed the options of sending an ambulance vs. having his wife drive him to the emergency department, which was approximately 20 minutes away from Jack's home. Jack felt confident he could keep himself safe during the drive, and his wife felt she could drive him safely. The therapist called both the on-call psychiatrist and the emergency department to inform them the patient would be arriving and to advise them regarding his current status. Jack arrived safely at the emergency department and was seen by the on-call psychiatrist.

In a study of response to suicidal patients in Californian EDs, Baraff and colleagues (2006) found that 23% of the EDs reported sending a patient home at times without receiving an evaluation from a mental health professional. Many did not have the capacity to admit to a psychiatric bed in their own facility, and the average waiting time in the ED for transfer to a psychiatric bed in another facility was 7 hours. The majority of EDs reported that the availability of outpatient mental health resources to follow-up discharged patients was a problem, underscoring the importance of clinicians making EDs aware of their availability.

The finding that a brief ED intervention combined with sustained follow-up reduced deaths by suicide (Fleischmann et al., 2008) and nonfatal suicide attempts (Stanley et al., 2018). emphasizes the importance for therapists to improve their links with EDs.

Clinical Pearl

Information a Clinician Needs to Have About Their Nearest Emergency Department

- What emergency department(s) is closest to your high-risk patients?
- What transportation is available to take your patient to the emergency department?
- What kind of mental health coverage exists in the emergency department?
- What is the protocol in the emergency department for responding to suicidal patients?
- Will the emergency department ask you to see your patient?
- Will the emergency department speak with you regarding disposition or providing follow-up appointments?

4.2.5 Psychiatric Emergency Services

It is critical for a clinician to have a clear understanding of their local psychiatric emergency service system

Another critical need for therapists is to have a clear understanding of the psychiatric emergency service system in their community. Communities vary greatly in the extent of psychiatric emergency resources available to them, so every therapist needs to have an understanding of this before commencing work with at-risk, suicidal patients. Psychiatric emergency services may operate out of a hospital or from a community mental health center, and services provided may include ED coverage, emergent appointments in the mental health center, phone/hotline capacity, or mobile outreach teams. Psychiatric emergency services may also have access to additional services such as hospital-based crisis beds, non-hospital-based crisis stabilization units, alternative forms of crisis housing, or peer support.

In most jurisdictions, emergency psychiatrists are the individuals with the most expertise in how to get someone at risk hospitalized. This will typically include knowledge of how to access a hospital bed for an individual from a population with specialized needs, such as children or the elderly. The best way, of course, for a clinician to be able to arrange a hospitalization is to have admitting privileges at a hospital or to have a close working relationship with a psychiatrist or other physician in order to arrange this. In many jurisdictions, the psychiatric emergency service may also be responsible for arranging involuntary hospitalizations.

4.2.6 Involuntary Hospitalization and the Use of the Police

The willingness and capacity of patients to keep themselves safe is a critical variable that needs to e considered before using involuntary interventions.

The willingness and the capacity of patients to collaborate in keeping themselves safe is a critical variable that needs to be considered before using involuntary interventions. The risks and benefits must be carefully assessed and documented as well as the patient's capacity and competence to enter into a collaborative plan to maintain his safety. For example, patients who are suicidal and intoxicated, or who are experiencing a psychotic episode as part of a schizophrenic or bipolar illness, or a delusional depression, may not have the capacity to collaboratively work to keep themselves safe. However, it must also be understood that the dispatching of police or ambulance against the patient's wishes is not always a benign intervention, regardless of the clinician's intentions. Such involuntary interventions may reduce imminent risk more dramatically than working with the patient collaboratively, but utilizing involuntary means is far from foolproof. The intervention may not be successful in bringing the patient to a secure setting, for example, the patient may flee the scene in advance of the police. At times the encounter is traumatic. If the patient does not agree to be transported, they may be restrained or put in handcuffs with risk of potential injury to all concerned. In addition, the use of coercion may damage the therapeutic relationship, sometimes beyond repair. Unfortunately, despite the life-and-death nature of these decisions, there is very little research to help guide clinicians in this decision-making. Amidst such uncertainty, knowledge of the patient's past behavior becomes particularly relevant.

It is a significant challenge when the clinician believes a patient is at high, imminent risk of suicide but the patient is unwilling to collaborate in receiving emergency care. In such instances, it is essential to understand state law and the available psychiatric emergency resources. Such high-stakes moments are not the time to begin learning how a system operates. Involuntary transport of patients at risk to EDs will often involve the utilization of police resources, and the ability of the police to intervene will typically vary from jurisdiction to jurisdiction. For example, some jurisdictions may require the police to personally observe evidence of dangerousness to self or others before intervening. The therapist's judgment, or statements made to the therapist, may not be sufficient in some circumstances to trigger involuntary transport.

4.2.7 Use of Mobile Crisis Outreach Services

Some jurisdictions will have a process as part of their psychiatric emergency response system that will allow a mobile crisis outreach team to be utilized in such situations. Mobile crisis outreach teams typically have the advantage of allowing for a suicide risk assessment to be done in the community, thereby avoiding the need for an involuntary transport for patients not found to be at high risk. It is often perplexing to patients, as well as to police, that at times a patient may be brought involuntarily to a hospital ED, only to be discharged from the ED several hours later.

However, there are numerous reasons that this can happen. EDs are responsible for making their own assessment of the patient once they enter the department. Risk can fluctuate over a period of hours, for example, as a blood alcohol level changes or as time passes from a stressful event. Also, the patient may have an incentive for concealing or minimizing the extent of their suicide risk upon interview in the ED in order to not be coerced to receive care. In addition, the ED may be influenced by issues such as lack of resources (e.g., a shortage of inpatient beds) that can lead to discharge from the ED, particularly when risk is ambiguous.

Mobile crisis outreach services can reduce the need for police intervention and involuntary transport

The use of mobile crisis outreach teams can reduce the likelihood of such situations. Rather than bringing patients to the ED for an evaluation, that evaluation can take place in the community. Mobile crisis outreach teams vary in their policies regarding going to private homes. Some insist on police accompaniment, so in some instances police involvement cannot be avoided, but the potential for being removed from one's home in handcuffs or restraints only to be released from the ED later can be minimized. In a national study, 39 states reported having implemented some form of mobile crisis services (Geller, Fisher, & McDermeit, 1995), although few had attempted any systematic evaluation of their impact. Several studies published since then have documented that mobile outreach teams may be effective as a diversion from psychiatric hospitalization.

Scott (2000) found that 55% of the emergencies handled by the mobile crisis team were managed without psychiatric hospitalization compared to 28% of the emergencies handled by regular police intervention – a statistically significant difference. In a study by Hugo and colleagues (2002), hospital-based emergency service contacts were found to be more than 3 times as likely to be admitted to a psychiatric inpatient unit when compared with those using a mobile community-based emergency service, regardless of their clinical characteristics. Similarly, a study by Dyches and colleagues (2002) of the impact of mobile crisis services on the use of mental health services found that, controlling for prior service use, mobile crisis intervention consumers with no prior mental health service use were 48% more likely to receive community-based mental health services within 90 days after the crisis event than a consumer receiving hospital-based interventions. Similarly, Currier and colleagues (2010) found that mobile outreach teams increased the frequency of suicidal patients discharged from the ED receiving outpatient mental health services.

It is very important to know whether your community has a mobile crisis outreach team available in these circumstances. The availability of such teams in communities in the United States varies widely. The need for every community to have access to a mobile crisis outreach team has been highlighted by the National Action Alliance for Suicide Prevention (2016) and the Substance Abuse and Mental Health Services Administration (2020).

4.3 Safety Planning

Central components of safety planning are involving family/ significant others, means restriction, and alternative coping behaviors

Safety planning is an important component of managing suicidal patients on an outpatient basis. Assisting the patient in maintaining their own safety is important both during a crisis and during ongoing treatment. The central components of safety planning typically include involving family or significant others, means restriction, and assisting the patient in utilizing alternative coping behaviors. The central components of safety planning are widely accepted as important suicide prevention measures. Reducing access to lethal means, decreasing isolation, and increasing support by involving family or friends, and promoting alternative coping behaviors are recommended by most authorities (Bongar, 2002; Linehan, 1993). However, there has been some confusion in the field because of the superficial similarities between this type of safety planning and the use of no-suicide contracts.

Safety plans (Stanley & Brown, 2012), called crisis response plans by Rudd and colleagues (2001), rely on providing instructions or assistance for the patient to help promote what they can do when in crisis, rather than relying solely on what they promise not to do. Two major recent studies have provided important information about the effectiveness of safety planning. In one study the safety planning was done in the emergency room, although one of the major advantages of safety planning is that it is a short intervention that can be done in many different settings including inpatient or outpatient or on a crisis hotline. In the SAFE VET study, a combination of collaborative safety planning and postdischarge telephone follow-up led to a reduction in suicidal behavior and to an increase in connection to mental health services by US veterans (Stanley et al., 2018). Bryan et al. (2017), in a study of crisis response planning in the US military, also found crisis response planning significantly reduced suicide attempts. The implication of having an intervention that can be delivered in multiple settings that does not require a full course of treatment is very significant.

Clinical Pearl
Denial of Suicidality: Cautions and Concerns

Clinicians often emphasize the patient's self-report regarding the presence or absence of suicidal thoughts. While this is clearly important information, it needs to be interpreted as part of a fuller assessment.

Self-report can be influenced by both mood and context, and when we ask patients to tell us that they will not attempt suicide over the next several days, we ask them to project into the future. The relationship between stated intent not to attempt suicide and the actual behavior, for example, for a patient who regularly abuses substances, can be tenuous indeed.

Busch and colleagues (2003) studied patients who died by suicide either in inpatient units or shortly after discharge. They found that a significant number denied/reported no suicidal ideation at their final clinical contact. The reported absence of suicidal ideation was therefore a poor predictor of short-term death by suicide, at least among patients in inpatient care. The precise reasons for this are not clear from the study. The influence of the context in which the assessment was taking place was one possibility. On an inpatient unit, reporting suicidal ideation can lead to continued hospitalization, at times involuntarily, and the potential for hospitalization can be a disincentive to honest disclosure. It is also possible that the patients were not suicidal at the time of the assessments but that their suicidality recurred, again underscoring how suicide risk can fluctuate over hours, days, or weeks.

4.3.1 Involving Family and Friends

> *An essential predicate to my emotional health was to reduce my isolation. Ironically, that very sense of alienation was perpetuated by having to live in a private world of suicidal thoughts that I could not share with anyone – or so I thought.* (Wise, 2012, p. 3)

Social isolation is a significant risk factor for suicide

Social isolation is a significant risk factor for suicide, a finding that is among the most robust in suicide prevention. Therefore, interventions that reduce social isolation hold promise for suicide prevention. Yet, even those with supportive persons in their lives can feel isolated, particularly if they have been unwilling to share what they are going through. Shea (2002) puts it eloquently, "Death is sometimes chosen as the only alternative by people who feel deeply alone or shamed, yet are profoundly loved and respected" (p. 5).

Encouraging self-disclosure of the depth of their pain and thoughts of suicide to significant others is therefore potentially important. Joiner (2005) has argued that failed belongingness and perceived burdensomeness are powerful risk factors for suicide. People need to feel connected to others and effective in those relationships: When they feel disconnected and alone, and a burden to others rather than a help, they may wish to die. Efforts need to be made to deal with these issues directly in treatment, both in ongoing therapy and during a crisis.

Potentially, a family session may help defuse a crisis and reduce risk. At minimum, family members need to be informed about how to access the clinician after hours or how to contact another 24-hour crisis service, such as a psychiatric emergency service or a suicide prevention hotline. This is particularly important given the research that those who make near lethal attempts are more likely to talk about suicide with families or friends than with healthcare professionals (Barnes et al., 2001).

Clinical Pearl
Components of Safety Planning

- Provide emergency phone numbers
- Reduce access to lethal means
- Involve family and friends
- Promote alternate coping techniques, including those that can be done alone and those that involve other people
- Review reasons for living
- Identify early warning signs of a developing crisis

In a crisis situation, families and significant others are often asked to provide a suicide watch, that is to constantly observe the suicidal person to prevent them from making a suicide attempt. Except under extreme circumstances, this is neither necessary nor recommended. A person who requires constant observation to maintain safety should be hospitalized.

Educating families regarding suicide risk is extremely important. Naturally, we all prefer to believe our loved ones are not in danger, particularly in the absence of obvious signs of danger. So, it is understandable for families to assume that when a relative is discharged from an inpatient psychiatric unit, they are no longer at risk, when in fact we know that this is a time of very high risk (Appleby et al., 1999). Similarly, families may misinterpret transient changes in mood as implying changes in longer term risk status. The fluctuating but often enduring nature of suicide risk must be emphasized. Families should be coached to be available, alert, and open to communication. Families may need assistance with their own emotional responses to the stress of knowing that their loved one is at risk.

Educating families regarding suicide risk is extremely important.

Education regarding warning signs should communicate what we know empirically as well as provide information that is patient specific. It is particularly important to communicate the need to take any discussion of suicide seriously. The willingness to ask directly about suicidal thoughts is critically important, along with instructions on how to respond if suicidal thoughts are present. If the patient and family feel that the presence of suicidal thoughts automatically mean there must be an inpatient hospitalization, there may be a disincentive for honest communication. Openness regarding suicidal thoughts, while quite difficult, also holds the potential for reducing isolation.

Clinical Pearl
Family Involvement Checklist

- Educate regarding suicide risk
- Encourage family to be willing to ask about suicidal thinking
- Discuss patient-specific warning signs
- Restrict lethal means
- Assure accessibility after hours
- Address perceived burdensomeness
- Enhance connectedness/reduce isolation

An extremely important reason to involve the family or significant others is to gain their assistance in reducing access to lethal means. It is far better to have a friend or family member remove a weapon from a patient's home, for example, rather than asking the patient to get a firearm out of the house, which would require them to handle the very weapon they are contemplating using to kill himself.

4.3.2 Means Restriction

Restriction to lethal means is one of the best validated suicide prevention strategies

The restriction of lethal means is one of the most frequently emphasized and best validated suicide prevention strategies, and it is particularly important during times of acute risk. Means restrictions strategies can be population-based or individualized clinical interventions. Barriers on bridges, carbon monoxide technologies, coal degasification, and paracetamol restrictions have shown impressive impacts on suicide mortality (Beautrais, 2007). Goal 6 of the National Strategy for Suicide Prevention is to promote efforts to reduce access to lethal means of suicide among individuals with identified suicide risk (US Department of Health and Human Services, 2012). This goal was included because of the strong evidence supporting such measures.

The reason that such strategies can be effective is that most people are ambivalent about dying by suicide and so many do not substitute alternative lethal methods. While the literature on the use of means restriction as a public health measure is robust, the literature on the clinical use of means restrictions strategies is not as well researched. However, based on the public health literature, clinical means restriction strategies should be considered to be based on a solid empirical foundation. A frequently used means restriction strategy, for example, is for prescribers of medication to manage the available amount of medication to prevent its use in a potentially lethal overdose. Another particularly important area of inquiry is the availability of firearms. It is important to ask about firearms availability, even if the patient has not indicated that it is a method of suicide they are thinking about. Firearms are highly lethal and, unlike some other means of suicide, the act cannot be aborted once it has begun. For example, a person may begin to ingest pills in a suicide attempt but in the process of overdosing decide that they do want to live. It is not uncommon on crisis lines to speak to people who have begun an overdose and stopped. Unfortunately, such second thoughts are not possible when firearms are used.

Additionally, instructing individuals or family members to reduce or eliminate access to lethal means is also a frequent recommendation, despite the challenges inherent in this task. However, there is some evidence supporting this clinical approach. For example, Kruesi and colleagues (1999) developed an approach for use in EDs, although the model could be easily adapted to other settings, including outpatient psychotherapy. They utilized a three-step method to educate parents of youth at high risk for suicide who received mental health assessments in EDs. The intervention could be accomplished in 5 minutes, even in busy emergency rooms. The three steps included informing parents that their adolescent was at risk for suicide and why the clinician thought so, telling the parents they can reduce the risk of suicide by getting firearms out of the house, and educating parents about different ways to dispose of or limit access to a firearm. Follow-up telephone interviews of parents indicated that exposure to the intervention resulted in a statistically significant increase in the self-reported restriction of means in the home.

One cannot presume that patients will automatically adhere to recommendations to remove lethal means. This is where the family may play a critical role. It is always preferable to have a family member or friend be the person who actually removes firearms or other lethal means. The clinician wants to avoid inadvertently creating a high-risk moment by having a suicidal person with a firearm in their hand. However, even family members may not adhere to recommendations to remove firearms. In a study by Brent and colleagues (2000), only 27% of parents of depressed adolescents were found to have removed firearms after having received a clinical recommendation to do so to reduce suicide risk. For this reason, a phone follow-up is strongly recommended. It is also important that clinicians do not allow their own personal feelings about guns to affect their clinical interventions. Many Americans greatly value gun ownership and adherence to clinical recommendations is likely to be poor if these views are not respected. A useful resource for clinicians about how to have conversations with patients about these difficult issues is *CALM: Counseling on Access to Lethal Means* available through https://www.sprc.org.

One cannot presume that patients will automatically adhere to recommendations to remove lethal means

A higher risk of suicide is associated with handguns compared to long guns, with unlocked more than locked guns, and with loaded more than unloaded guns (Brent, 2001). Simon (2007), in a review of the principles of gun safety management, recommended that clinicians inquire about guns at home or located outside the home (e.g., car, office, etc.) when working with suicidal patients. They should also ask if their patient intends to purchase or obtain a firearm. When firearms need to be removed, it is recommended that the patient designate a willing, responsible person to remove and secure guns and ammunition to a location outside the home that is unknown to the patient, and that the clinician confirms with the designated person that the firearms and ammunition have been removed. Simon further recommends that patients in EDs and inpatient units not be discharged until this is accomplished (Simon, 2007). Transfer of firearms to a family member or friend needs to be done with an awareness of relevant laws within the jurisdiction which may preclude this. In some jurisdictions in the United States a family member can seek a court order for temporary removal of firearms. There is suggestive evidence that jurisdictions with extreme risk protective orders have had an impact on the prevalence of suicide. However, in many instances an individual at risk or their family members may be unwilling to consider removing firearms from the home, so it is important to be aware of options to promote safe storage within the home. A randomized control trial of Mississippi National Guard members found that a brief lethal means counseling intervention and the provision of cable locks improved safe storage of firearms over treatment as usual up to 6 months after the intervention (Anestis et al., 2020).

4.3.3 Safety Planning Versus No-Suicide Contracts

Suicide is not beholden to an evening's promises, nor does it always hearken to plans drawn up in lucid moments and banked in good intentions. (Jamison, 1999)

One of the most controversial areas in the treatment of suicidal persons is the use of no-suicide contracts. No- suicide contracts are also sometimes referred to as no-harm contracts, safety contracts, or suicide prevention contracts. Despite the lack of evidence to support their efficacy as a suicide prevention technique, their use is reportedly widespread. According to an IOM report, "Suicide prevention contracts are widely used in all mental health settings as risk management tools, but they remain poorly evidenced" (Institute of Medicine et al., 2002, p. 291). In her 2007 review, Lewis describes suicide contracts as "standard practice in the treatment of suicidal ideation" (Lewis, 2007, p. 50). In their basic form, no-suicide contracts are simply promises not to kill oneself.

No-suicide contracts can be verbal or written. When written, they typically include a statement in which the patient agrees not to attempt suicide. Written contracts are typically signed by both the patient and therapist.

They may include an alternative that the patient agrees to engage in when feeling suicidal, such as calling their therapist or a suicide prevention hotline (Lewis, 2007).

Despite the lack of evidence supporting their use, no-suicide contracts must serve functions for clinicians or they would not be used so widely and so often. The IOM further reports, "…there is a general perception that they are helpful" (Institute of Medicine et al., 2002, p. 291). To understand this, we should examine the context in which these contracts are typically used. Most frequently, these are used when there are circumstances leading to concerns about increased risk, and there is a need to decide upon an intervention to respond to this increased risk.

No-suicide contracts provide a straightforward technique for making a complex, clinical judgment, a judgment often fraught with anxiety and uncertainty. If the suicidal person is willing to "contract for safety," they are likely to be treated as an outpatient. If they are not willing, then hospitalization is the answer. Frequently, the consequence of refusal to agree to a no-suicide contract may be involuntary hospitalization (Lewis, 2007). There may be motivation to go along with such contracts in order to avoid unwanted outcomes. Obtaining a no-suicide contract may therefore reduce a clinician's anxiety, but it may also play an inordinately influential role in clinical decision-making. This is of particular concern given Farrow and colleagues' (2002) finding that clients tended to experience no-suicide contracts as a barrier to talking about their suicidal thoughts. Thus, rather than assisting clients to talk openly about their thoughts, allowing clinicians to make a more informed estimate of suicide risk and collaboratively make a decision about the need for hospitalization, no-suicide contracts may inadvertently encourage concealment by the client and a less informed and thorough risk assessment by the clinician. This may be particularly problematic if contracts are a substitute for more empirically justifiable interventions, such as addressing means restriction or involving the family. No-suicide contracts are typically used as a justification for outpatient treatment or for readiness for discharge from inpatient units or EDs.

No-suicide contracts are not part of the formal written tradition of suicide assessment. More often their use is perpetuated by word of mouth and clinicians have not received formal training in their use. Their popularity may well reflect the absence of training in suicide risk assessment and treatment experienced by many of the mental health professions (Institute of Medicine et al., 2002)

Refusal to sign such a contract does not mean a patient is at imminent risk, nor does agreement mean that risk is lessened (Institute of Medicine et al., 2002). Patients' motivations for signing or refusing to sign a contract are complex, and one risk of using no-suicide contracts is that they may provide a false sense of security to the clinician and cause lessened diligence about the possibility of suicide (Simon, 1999).

Agreement to no suicide contracts are often heavily influenced by the potential consequences of refusal

One risk of using no-suicide contracts is that they may provide a false sense of security

Part of the confusion around no-suicide contracts involves the recognition that these techniques combine suicide prevention techniques that are misguided with those that are valuable. For example, a competent assessment must explore whether the patient intends to die by suicide. Attempting to gain a commitment to work on staying alive is a component of empirically supported treatments such as DBT. When no-suicide contracts include elements of a safety plan, such as provision of a phone number to call when feeling suicidal and removal of potentially lethal means such as firearms from the patient's environment or the involvement of family or significant others to form a supportive network around the patient, they may be of real value.

The dilemma is in relying solely on the patient's promise that they will not attempt to kill themselves rather than implementing a comprehensive safety plan. Promises to not attempt suicide, even when given in good faith, assume the patient can accurately anticipate the recurrence and intensity of their suicidal urges. Particularly for those with substance abuse problems or psychotic symptoms, this can be extremely difficult.

According to the Minnesota Office of Ombudsman for Mental Health and Developmental Disabilities (2002), no-suicide contracts were in place for almost every suicide that occurred in an inpatient, acute care facility. Other studies have also found that a significant number of those who made suicide attempts or died by suicide had such contracts in place at the time of their suicidal act (APA, 2003).

No-suicide contracts should never be used in place of appropriate suicide risk assessment and treatment

In a clinical trial in which crisis response planning was directly compared to no-suicide contracts in the US military crisis response planning (safety planning) was found to reduce suicide attempts by 76% (Bryan et al., 2017).

4.4 Treatment Techniques

4.4.1 Treatment Targets

Most treatments for suicidal persons advocate some form of targeting for pursuing work in therapy. The therapist must have a clear idea of how to proceed and what must be prioritized. Shneidman believes that the implications of the ten commonalities of suicide for psychotherapy are to "reduce the pain, remove the blinders, lighten the pressure" (Shneidman, 1996, p. 139). As suicide is an effort to escape from unendurable pain, reducing the pain is a crucial priority. Any lessening of the pain may assist in making the intolerable tolerable. Both promoting change and enhancing acceptance can be viable

Treatment targets help clinicians prioritize

means for doing this. Problem solving pressing and painful problems may successfully reduce the pressure and thus the press towards suicide. Alternatively, pain can at times be reduced through acceptance, by no longer struggling to resist a reality that cannot be changed.

In DBT, treatment targets are set according to a defined hierarchy. This hierarchy is determined not by how many weeks or months of treatment have taken place, but instead by the behaviors in which the patient is engaging. Suicidal behavior is always the first priority, and nothing else can be addressed in individual therapy sessions until the suicidal behavior is thoroughly analyzed. If no suicidal behavior has taken place, the second priority is therapy-interfering behavior (Linehan, 1993). This is any behavior, by either patient or therapist, that threatens the therapeutic relationship. The notion here is that therapy is frequently terminated by either the patient or the therapist when one of them unilaterally becomes frustrated and ends the treatment. Therefore, any interactions that threaten the treatment must be thoroughly examined. If neither suicidal behavior nor therapy-interfering behavior are present, the next target is quality of life interfering behaviors, behaviors that while not life threatening, make a life worth living impossible, for example substance abuse.

4.4.2 Skills Training

Skills training as a therapeutic means for reducing the risk of suicidal behavior has been most extensively developed in DBT. In DBT, skills training is a central focus with patients expected to participate in a weekly skills training group throughout a year of treatment. The goal is to help patients actively problem-solve life's challenges using an array of skills. There is a focus in DBT on assisting the patient in acquiring skills, strengthening skills, and in generalizing skills to differing situations and contexts (Linehan, 1993). Acquiring new skills is the focus of the skills training group using didactic instruction, role plays, and other methods.

While individual therapy can also be a setting for such instruction, for people in suicidal crisis it may be difficult to systematically attend in individual therapy to such skills training. The goal in individual therapy is to get the patient to utilize the skills they are learning in the group.

DBT skills training includes modules on mindfulness, emotional regulation, interpersonal effectiveness, and distress tolerance

The DBT skills training modules (mindfulness, interpersonal effectiveness, emotional regulation, and distress tolerance) are presented sequentially, and the teaching of the skills is the most important task during the conduct of the group. Thus, a patient who began to speak about suicide during the group would not become the focus of attention. The group therapist would guide the group back to the teaching of skills through a comment such as, "I understand that you're feeling suicidal right now, but that underscores for me the importance of you learning these skills and being able to use them to have a life worth living."

Of the four types of skills taught in DBT, mindfulness is likely the least familiar to clinicians. Influenced by Eastern philosophy, mindfulness focuses on cultivating an awareness of the present moment. Mindfulness skills also build on the central insight that while we can control what we do, we have very limited control over what we think and feel. We do not decide what thought we will have nor do we decide what emotion we will experience. Yet we tend to identify ourselves with our thoughts and emotions, and we overestimate the extent to which our thoughts and feelings are under conscious control. We can, however, learn to control what we pay attention to. For millennia, techniques such as meditation and yoga have been used to enhance this attentional control. In addition to Linehan's work, using mindfulness with chronically suicidal persons who met diagnostic criteria for borderline personality disorder, mindfulness has also now been utilized in the treatment of depression (Teasdale et al., 2000). Examples of the mindfulness skills taught in DBT include observing, a process that involves the skill of observing the inner flow of experience. Another example is describing experience rather than judging it. For example, "my boss treated me terribly" would be a judgment. In contrast, "my boss shouted at me" would be a description.

The importance of mindfulness as a fundamental skill in DBT is underscored by returning to review mindfulness skills after each of the other skills training modules is completed. In many ways, cultivation of mindfulness stands in direct opposition to the desire to die by suicide. Shneidman described the common goal in suicide to be the cessation of consciousness and the ending of awareness; in contrast, mindfulness aims to enhance conscious awareness. While it is not yet known what role mindfulness skills play in DBT's effectiveness, its potential seems clear. (See Witkiewitz and colleagues, 2017, for a short, user-friendly and clinically oriented introduction to mindfulness.)

Mindfulness stands in direct opposition to the desire to die by suicide

Distress tolerance includes two components: One component focuses on crisis survival skills while the other attempts to teach deeper forms of acceptance. Crisis survival skills involve techniques designed to help the suicidal person get through the crisis without resorting to self-destructive behavior. They are not designed to solve the problems that are leading a person to be suicidal in the first place, rather they are intended to help the person stay alive long enough to have a chance to solve those problems. Various forms of distraction would be examples of crisis survival strategies. For instance, holding an ice cube in the hand and focusing on the intense sensation of cold can be a potential distractor from suicidal urges. In fact, a recent study by Stanley and colleagues (2021) found that distraction-based techniques were best at lowering the intensity of suicidal thoughts. The other component of distress tolerance skills involves accessing deeper levels of acceptance: Linehan (1993) calls this practice "radical acceptance."

Crisis survival skills help the suicidal person get through the crisis without resorting to self-destructive behavior

Emotional regulation skills blend teaching about the nature of emotions based on current scientific research, with the learning of skills that can help change emotional experiences through behavior change. For example, the skill of opposite action involves exposure principles, such as approaching what you fear and being open and not hiding when experiencing shame.

Interpersonal effectiveness skills are perhaps the most familiar for clinicians, incorporating elements of treatments such as assertiveness training while maintaining an emphasis on "doing what's effective."

Rudd and colleagues (2001) emphasize the importance of skill building in their time-limited cognitive behavioral therapy as well, identifying emotional regulation, distress tolerance, and self-monitoring to be core interventions that should be standard in working with suicidal patients regardless of the specifics of the clinical presentation.

4.4.3 Self-Monitoring/Homework Assignments

The importance of homework assignments, like that of telephone interventions, rests on an understanding that the goal of therapy is to enhance the patient's ability to cope with suicidal thoughts and urges in their day-to- day life outside of the therapy session.

Both DBT and CBT incorporate the use of homework assignments. In DBT, the skills training group exposes patients systematically to the skills of mindfulness, interpersonal effectiveness, emotional regulation, and distress tolerance, and assigns homework to practice the skills that have been taught each week. The individual therapist has the task of encouraging and persuading the patient to use these skills in their daily life. In order to be able to utilize these skills in a suicidal crisis it is essential that patients have practiced them when they are not emotionally overwhelmed. In DBT, skills training commences at the very start of treatment. In CBT, there is an emphasis first on cognitive modification, and then on skills development, with homework assignments being utilized for both.

Both Rudd and colleagues (2001) and Linehan (1993) emphasize the importance of self-monitoring. Rudd and colleagues recommend the use of a treatment log in which the patient makes entries at the end of each session. In DBT, the patient fills out a diary card on a daily basis. The diary cards include ratings of the intensity of suicidal ideation/urges, as well as whether suicidal behavior occurs. The use of skills being taught in the skills training group is also recorded. Review of the diary cards is the first task in individual therapy each week. If suicidal behavior has taken place, it becomes the immediate focus of the session. In DBT, patients are required, when they have engaged in

Clinical Vignette 10

Chain Analysis of Suicidal Behavior

Janet was a 27-year-old female who cut her wrists following an upsetting encounter in the department store in which she worked. At her next therapy session after she had cut her wrists, she worked together with her therapist to identify the chain of events, both external and internal, that had led to her self-destructive act. They then reviewed skills she could have utilized as alternatives at each step.

Chain Analysis	Solution Analysis
Argument with customer in store	Interpersonal effectiveness skills
Thinks, "I can't stand this anymore"	Distress tolerance/radical acceptance
Quits job and leaves store	Interpersonal effectiveness skills
Thinks, "I've failed again" and feels ashamed	Describing rather than judging, mindfulness
Goes to car and cuts self with razor	Distraction/crisis survival skills

suicidal behavior, to fill out a detailed, behavioral chain analysis of the episode examining vulnerability factors, precipitating events, and consequences of the suicidal behavior. For an example of a chain analysis of suicidal behavior, see Clinical Vignette 10. The patient therefore develops an increasing awareness of what leads to and reinforces their suicidal behavior, rather than experiencing the suicidal behavior as coming out of the blue in a sudden rush of emotion. At each step of the chain that leads to the suicidal behavior, specific action steps are identified that can be used in the future as alternative more skillful behaviors that can be utilized. This is referred to as a solution analysis.

In a solution analysis, specific action steps are identified that can be used as alternatives to suicidal behavior

4.4.4 Cognitive Interventions

Most cognitive behavioral therapies include a similar range of interventions, although they may vary in the emphasis given to specific interventions. All cognitive behavioral treatments contain cognitive interventions, but in some approaches, such as Rudd and colleagues (2001) and Brown and colleagues (2006), these interventions are more central. The private meaning assigned by the suicidal individual to their experience and the core beliefs about self, other, and the world, are each imbued with some level of hopelessness. Regardless of the specific personal meaning, Rudd and colleagues (2001) recommend a core set of techniques to use to modify the suicidal belief system. They captured this approach in the acronym ICARE:

Identify	Identifying the automatic thoughts and core beliefs
Connect	Connect these thoughts to cognitive distortions
Assess	Assess or evaluate the evidence for thesebeliefs
Restructure	Constructing a more realistic belief
Execute	Act as though the new belief is true, performing a behavioral experiment to disconfirm the original dysfunctional belief

Although DBT focuses on the role of behavior and emotion, rather than on cognitions, it also includes cognitive modification procedures, although they are used more informally and less systematically than in Rudd's model. Clarifying current contingencies is an example of a cognitive technique used in DBT. Recognizing the negative consequences of suicide attempts would be another example of this technique. Suicide attempts typically serve a function in the short run (e.g., they help the patient escape pain), but these attemptscause more problems in the long run and are thus counterproductive. Helping patients understand this is an example of clarifying current contingencies.

4.4.5 Exposure Treatment

Linehan has also identified the role of exposure-based techniques in treating suicidal behavior (Linehan, 1993). For patients with borderline personality disorder, almost any intense emotional experience may trigger suicidal behavior in an effort to escape the emotional intensity. More broadly, suicidal behavior can be conceptualized as escape or avoidance behavior, an effort to block or get away from experiences that seem intolerable. For chronically suicidal patients, this can be almost an automatic response. Suicidal ideation itself can have this function. The thought of suicide reduces, at least momentarily, the experience of painful emotions, and suicidal thinking is thus reinforced and more likely to be repeated. To change this automatic response requires the painful emotion to be experienced while blocking the escape that the thought of suicide provides. This can be worked on repeatedly during the therapy session. For an example of exposure techniques in practice, see Clinical Vignette 11.

Clinical Vignette 11
Exposure Techniques in Practice

Therapist: It sounds like it was a very difficult weekend.
Patient: It was.
Therapist: You were very upset your son didn't call.
Patient: I'm feeling suicidal.
Therapist: You're feeling suicidal right now?
Patient: Yes.
Therapist: When did you start to think about suicide?
Patient: Just a minute ago.
Therapist: What was happening just before you started thinking about suicide?
Patient: When you mentioned my son.
Therapist: When I mentioned you were very upset that your son didn't call, you immediately began to think about suicide?
Patient: Yes.
Therapist: What I would like to do now is to repeat what I had said, and what I would like you to do is to try to focus on observing the feelings that you have in response and then describe them to me. This is part of helping you cope with intense feelings without becoming suicidal. Is that OK?
Patient: I'll try.
Therapist: Here goes. You were very upset when your son didn't call over the weekend.
Patient: Yes.
Therapist: What did you notice that you felt when I said that?
Patient: I felt very angry.

4.4.6 Reducing Perceived Burdensomeness

Perceived burdensomeness is an important risk factor for suicide (Joiner, 2005). According to Joiner it is one of the most important reasons people want to kill themselves. When patients are at increased risk and perceive they are a burden to others, particularly to loved ones, they may believe that death by suicide will remove that burden from them. While it is true that mental illness can have an impact on friends and family, and that chronic mental illness in particular may impose some burdens, it is rare that this burden will be greater than the lifelong burden carried by loved ones who have experienced a death by suicide. Addressing perceived burdensomeness is complicated by the fact that suicidal behavior itself creates burden for caretakers. In an important study of the impact of current suicidal ideation and past suicide attempts by bipolar patients on caregiver burden, caregivers for suicidal patients with suicidal histories had greater burden and poorer health than caregivers for bipolar patients without such histories (Chessick et al., 2007). Suicide attempts in particular seemed to have a strong impact. The suicide attempt of a spouse or family member is an experience that can have enduring effects for years to come. Such complexities need to be kept in mind when dealing with these issues clinically. The patient's perception that they are a burden may be at least partially true, so simple reassurance that the patient is not a burden may be insufficient and lack credibility. At the same time, it may be the pain of almost losing a loved one to suicide and living with that fear over time that creates such a burden. However, the response of survivors' when such fears come to pass is more likely to be devastation than relief. So, the key therapeutic task may be to help the patient recognize that while there may be some burden that is imposed on family by their illness, the magnitude of that burden pales in comparison to the burdens experienced by loved ones following a death by suicide.

A key therapeutic task is to help the suicidal person recognize the devastation experienced by loved ones following a death by suicide

An excellent example of the use in psychotherapy of helping a suicidal person grasp the depth of the devastation their suicide would create comes from Terry Wise's account (2003) of her near fatal suicide attempt, and her psychotherapy both before and after the attempt. Terry recounts how her therapist systematically and relentlessly led her through the impact her suicide would have on all those she loved. This was not easy work: "I hated having to say the words that brought the horrid consequences to life" (Wise, 2012).

The goal is not to make the suicidal person feel guilty or to persuade them that they ought to live in order to spare other's feelings, but rather to help them cast a clear, realistic eye on the actual consequences of their suicide and to break down the tunnel vision and cognitive constriction characteristic of the suicidal mind.

Again, from Wise's account, "...the intensity was necessary in order to shake the roots of my long-standing beliefs. This was the first time I felt my rationalization no one would be seriously affected by my suicide being jeopardized" (2012, p. 137).

"This was the first time I felt my rationalization no one would be seriously affected by my suicide being jeopardized" (Terry Wise)

Clinical Pearl
Strategies for Addressing Perceived Burdensomeness

Sustained psychotherapeutic exploration of the potential impact of the patient's suicide on others

Family session to explore burdensomeness

Normalization by comparison with physical illness

Sharing of the survivor literature

Another technique is to normalize the experience of burden by equating it to physical illness. Diabetes and heart disease pose burdens on families as well but far less than the patient's death would impose.

Finally, the survivor literature can be utilized to help the suicidal patient achieve a more balanced understanding of what their death by suicide would mean to those they love. Books such as *My Son, My Son* by Iris Bolton (1984) clearly underscore the depth of pain caused by suicide.

4.4.7 Failed Belongingness

Joiner (2005) proposes, based on his review of the scientific literature, that the two major reasons people want to kill themselves are that they perceive themselves as a burden to others and that they feel that they do not belong. The notion that social integration protects against suicide, while social isolation intensifies risk, is one of the oldest findings in suicidology (Durkheim, 1897/1951). It is also noteworthy that social withdrawal is frequently experienced in depression. While feeling connected to family, friends, and community is protective against suicide, this protection is not absolute, as desire for suicide can also be intensified by feeling like a burden to those one loves. Nevertheless, promoting social connection and a sense of belonging should be considered an important goal of psychotherapy.

For persons at risk in therapy, the connection to the therapist is extremely important for suicide prevention, and it underscores the importance of being able to rapidly establish a collaborative relationship. However, as important as the relationship with the therapist is, it is not a replacement for an enduring connection and sense of belonging with family, friends, and community. A potentially useful strategy to promote connection and belongingness is to assess what the client's most important values in life have been and provide assistance in connecting or reconnecting with organizations that may share those values (e.g., churches, social causes). This can lead not only to a greater sense of belonging, but also to a greater sense of effectiveness. For many people at risk for suicide, previous meaningful relationships may have faded. Reconnecting with family and friends who were once valued relationships can be a very important intervention.

4.4.8 Bibliotherapy and Online Sources

There are a number of ways in which bibliotherapy can be of benefit. These could be manuals that help with the implementation of specific therapies, or stories of people with lived experience of suicide loss or suicidal crisis that can promote healing. Both CBT and DBT (Ellis & Newman, 1996; Linehan, 1993) provide a manual to aid patients with utilizing the skills and techniques provided in therapy sessions. Such materials help support both approaches and emphasis on homework assignments promote practice of coping skills outside of sessions. Such aids serve an important bridging function, so that patients do not have to rely solely on their memory of instructions or advice given in psychotherapy sessions. In addition, bibliotherapy focused on the diagnostic conditions that may be precipitating a suicidal crisis, such as psychoeducational books on depression, bipolar disorder, or substance abuse, can also be of value.

Another potential use of bibliotherapy relates to the issue of perceived burdensomeness as a risk factor, as emphasized by Joiner (2005). Frequently patients, particularly those who have been struggling with a mental illness over a period of time, will experience themselves as being a burden to their family or loved ones. With the cognitive constriction typical of suicidal persons, they are frequently unaware of the devastating burden that their suicide would impose on all those who care about them, or else rationalize that the pain caused by their mental illness or other problems outweighs the pain that would be caused by their suicide. This is rarely true. To attempt to change this misperception, it can be helpful to recommend readings from the survivor literature (see Box 8). This poignant literature provides accounts of deaths by suicide from the perspective of bereaved family members, describing the anguish that they have experienced. Being familiar with this literature, which presents the experience of loss from the perspective of parent, sibling, spouse etc, can allow the clinician to expose the person considering suicide to a far more realistic view of the likely impact on their loved ones if they go through with the lethal act. Presentation of this material needs to be handled sensitively. The intent is not simply to try to make the patient feel guilty for considering suicide, but rather to give them a clearer perspective on what their death would actually mean. While these books are typically written to help other survivors cope, and are highly recommended for use by therapists for that purpose, they can be of help to the suicidal person themselves.

Box 8
Family Survivor Literature

- *My Son...My Son: A Guide to Healing After Death, Loss, or Suicide* (1984) by Iris Bolton with C. Mitchell (parent survivor)
- *No Time to Say Goodbye: Surviving the Suicide of a Loved One* (1999) by Carla Fine (spouse survivor)
- *Do They Have Bad Days in Heaven? Surviving the Suicide Loss of a Sibling* (2001) by Michelle Linn-Gust (sibling survivor)
- *Touched by Suicide: Hope and Healing After Suicide* (2006) by Mike Meyers and Carla Fine (spouse survivor)
- *After a Suicide: A Workbook for Grieving Kids* (2001) by The Dougy Center (child survivor)

Books that recount the experience of going through a suicidal crisis and emerging ultimately with a life worth living can also be valuable (see Box 9). Such books, by people who know what it is like to face this dark night of the soul, promote hope. *Waking Up*, by Terry Wise, can be of particular value for psychotherapy patients as her relationship with her therapist is a central part of the book. For families dealing with a suicidal adolescent, the book *Will's Choice* presents the experience of an adolescent who makes a near lethal suicide attempt from the point of view of his mother (Griffith, 2005).

Box 9
Survivors of Suicidal Crises Literature

- *Night Falls Fast* (1999) by Kay Redfield Jamison
- *Waking Up* (2012) by Terry Wise
- *Eight Stories Up* (2008) by De Quincy Lezine
- *Darkness Visible* (1990) by William Styron
- *Will's Choice* (2005) by Gail Griffith
- *Children of Jonah* (2001) by James Clemons (Ed.)
- *Manual for Support Groups for Suicide Attempt Survivors* (2014) Didi Hirsch Mental Health Services Suicide Prevention Center

4.4.9 Outreach and Follow-Up

When therapy comes to a planned conclusion, it is useful to schedule one or two additional sessions several months after therapy has ended. These return visits may function as booster sessions where the patient's coping can be reviewed, recurrence of suicidality can be assessed for, and the use of skillful alternatives to suicidal behavior can be reinforced.

An excellent brief intervention that can be used following both planned and premature terminations from treatment is the use of brief, caring letters. This approach was first studied by Motto and Bostrum (Motto & Bostrum, 2001). Patients hospitalized for suicide risk were contacted 30 days after discharge. Those patients who had either refused or discontinued therapy were randomized to either an experimental or control condition. The intervention was a brief letter sent to them by a researcher who had interviewed them while they were hospitalized. The note simply said:

> Dear ______________,
> It has been a while since you were here at the hospital, and we hope things are going well for you. If you wish to drop us a note, we would be glad to hear from you.

A self-addressed, unstamped envelope was enclosed, and if the person wrote back, their letter was answered. After 2 years, the experimental group that had received the letters had significantly fewer suicides than the control, no-contact group. While at the 5-year follow-up this effect was no longer statistically significant, the study provides strong support for the value of routinely incorporating such letters into treatment of high-risk suicidal patients, particularly those that drop out of treatment. The results of the ED follow-up study by Fleischmann and colleagues (2008) also provide support that episodic but sustained contact may have great value.

A similar study was conducted by Carter and colleagues (2005). Patients who presented to an ED with deliberate self-poisoning (intentional overdoses) received a nondemanding postcard (enclosed in an envelope) at set intervals, between 30 days and twelve months after the suicide attempt. While there were not any differences in the proportion of patients in the two groups who made repeat attempts, the number of repeat attempts was reduced by 50% in the experimental group. There was also a significant decrease in the number of used hospital days associated with the decrease in the number of attempts.

Brief, caring letters should become a standard part of practice with suicidal patients

Combined, the results of the Motto and Bostrum (2001) and the Carter and colleagues (2005) studies provide persuasive evidence that high-risk patients who drop out of treatment, and are unable to be re-engaged by telephone outreach, should receive nondemanding letters periodically. Given the low-risk, low-cost nature of the intervention, combined with the large potential benefit, such letters should become a standard part of practice with suicidal patients.

The critical importance of proactive outreach and follow-up has also been established in two recent controlled trials that involved telephonic follow-up of suicidal patients following discharge from ERs. The Safe Vet study (Stanley et al., 2018) showed a combination of safety planning and telephonic follow-up reduced suicide attempts, and the ED-SAFE study (Miller et al., 2017) showed universal screening and telephone follow-up reduced suicide attempts with the follow-up the critical factor.

4.4.10 Postvention

Responding to the Aftermath of Suicide Attempts

Finding empathy for a suicide attempt is as unlikely as killing your parents and receiving sympathy for being an orphan.
(Terry Wise, 2012, p. 131)

In addition to the need for crisis intervention in the immediate aftermath of a suicide attempt, which includes the need for medical evaluation and a suicide risk assessment to determine whether psychiatric hospitalization is necessary, suicide attempts have consequences and implications that must be thoroughly explored in ongoing psychotherapy.

These consequences range from the impact of the suicide attempt on the therapy relationship, the impact on family and friends, potential impact on job status and financial status, as well as the effect on the individual's sense of self-efficacy and self-esteem. The suicide attempt also has implications that must be explored to prevent future suicide attempts. There is a need to thoroughly analyze all the steps leading to the suicide attempt to determine how alternative solutions can be promoted in the future. Each possible turning point on the road to the suicide attempt must be identified. Linehan (1993), as previously described, utilizes a behavioral chain analysis combined with a solution analysis to accomplish this.

Suicide attempts are powerful interpersonal events that must be understood and coped with

In *Waking Up*, Terry Wise provides a compelling example of a therapist and a client grappling with the aftermath of a suicide attempt. Understanding the impact on family and friends can also be crucial. Suicide attempts are powerful interpersonal events that set off reverberations that must be understood and coped with. If not addressed in therapy, suicide attempts can lead either to increased isolation, if no one is able to talk about what has happened, or increased conflict, if the suicide attempt is experienced by others as either an expression of anger towards them or a sign that the suicidal individual doesn't care about the family.

A suicide attempt should always lead to a re-evaluation of the treatment plan

A suicide attempt should also lead to a re-evaluation of the treatment plan. While the fact that a suicide attempt took place does not always mean that the treatment plan needs to be changed, particularly if suicide risk is already clearly and comprehensively being addressed in the treatment plan, a suicide attempt should always lead to a review so that the clinician can see if they can identify anything being missed.

Communication of stories of hope has a positive impact on suicide risk

A significant advance in suicide prevention has been the willingness of people who have attempted suicide or who have experienced a suicidal crisis to share their stories of hope and recovery. In addition to helping to foster a culture of openness and acceptance regarding mental health, there is evidence that the communication of such stories of hope in the media has a positive impact on suicide risk, what has been referred to as the Papageno effect. There are now websites and resources that can help provide such needed mutual support. Examples are https://livethroughthis.org and https://www.nowmattersnow.org.

Responding to Deaths by Suicide

Undoubtedly, losing a patient to suicide is one of the most difficult and traumatic events that therapists can experience in their professional lives. Like all survivors of suicide, the therapist is likely to experience both powerful and conflicting emotions. Also, like all survivors of suicide, therapists are likely to ask themselves many questions about their own actions prior to the death.

However, the therapist's efforts to work through their own grief and doubt may be complicated by processes of administrative review and concerns about legal liability For years, systematic review of deaths by suicide in mental health treatment have been relatively rare, which is likely a reflection of the more generalized difficulty in talking about suicide that afflicts our entire society. However, organizations such as the Joint Commission and the Veterans Healthcare Administration have now mandated root cause analyses of deaths by suicide. The heart of a root cause analysis is to look for systems issues that can be learned from and corrected rather than to identify personal fault or blame. For therapists working outside of organized healthcare delivery system, a similar root cause analysis should be undertaken within the context of a group practice or supervision group. State law should be consulted to determine whether in the clinician's locality this is subject to legal discovery. The death of a patient by suicide does not necessarily mean that a therapist has done something wrong, just as a death during surgery does not necessarily mean that a surgeon made a mistake during the surgery. However, we owe it to all those we treat, as well as their families, to routinely review all deaths by suicide that occur while in treatment, to maximize what we can learn and how we can improve our practice in order to better help others.

We owe it to all those we have lost, as well as to their families, to review all deaths by suicide that occur while in treatment

A particularly important question is how to respond to the family of the person who has died by suicide. If the therapist has already involved them in the treatment, they will not be strangers. But if not, this could be the therapist's first contact. Bennett and colleagues (2006) emphasize that a therapist's actions should be governed by whether the therapist can be of benefit to the family.

> When permitted by state law, you may discuss some of the general therapeutic issues with the patient's family, share your condolences, and try to give the family a sense of closure. Not only is this the humane thing to do, it also reduces your risk of being sued if you are open, caring, and forthright with the family. (Bennett et al., 2006. p. 170)

Referring family members or close friends to a group for survivors of suicide should be considered

As part of these discussions with the family, providing resources to assist the family in coping with the immensity of their loss may be appropriate. In some communities, survivors of suicide groups exist in which the surviving family members can be supported by others who understand the enormity of the pain they are experiencing. Information on survivor of suicide groups is available from national suicide prevention groups such as the American Association of Suicidology (https://suicidology.org), or the American Foundation for Suicide Prevention (https://afsp.org), among others.

Referral for therapy may also be appropriate. Clinicians who survive the loss of a client should refer the surviving family members to colleagues (Dunne, 1992).

4.5 Mechanisms of Action

The research evidence in the suicide prevention literature is not robust enough to specify with certainty the mechanisms of action for programs with some evidence of effectiveness. Many of the approaches with some evidence of success have utilized multiple component interventions. For example, it is unknown if the effectiveness of the Air Force Suicide Prevention Program, which reduced suicide by 33%, was due to the promotion of a culture of shared responsibility for intervening with those at risk for suicide, which may have reduced social isolation and enhanced belongingness, to the encouragement of help seeking, to the universal accessibility of healthcare services, or to some combination of these factors (Knox et al., 2003). The program's success in also reducing episodes of serious domestic violence, accidental deaths, and homicides suggests that the program had an impact on shared risk and protective factors across these different, severe problems.

Similarly, the effectiveness of DBT in a randomized control trial was in response to a multicomponent intervention, making it unclear which components or combination of components were essential and which were not. For example, are all four of the types of skills taught in DBT (mindfulness, emotional regulation, interpersonal effectiveness, and distress tolerance) equally important? The lesson that may be drawn is that suicide prevention requires more complex, multidimensional approaches that impact the person's life in multiple spheres.

DBT can be divided into acceptance and change strategies

The strategies utilized in DBT can be divided into acceptance and change strategies. We are used to thinking of psychotherapeutic interventions as efforts at change, and Linehan (1993) has pointed out that much of behavior therapy is really a technology of change. Emphasis on acceptance strategies has been much more recent. In DBT, skills training modules in mindfulness and distress tolerance are considered acceptance strategies while modules in emotional regulation and interpersonal effectiveness are considered change strategies. Distress tolerance strategies include skills focusing on surviving the crisis, not solving the underlying problems but, simply and profoundly, staying alive until the intensity of the wish to die diminishes. Another example of an acceptance skill is radical acceptance. Much in life cannot be changed, it can only be accepted. The death of a loved one and traumas that took place in the past are examples of events that can only be accepted, they cannot be changed.

While the precise balance between acceptance and change responsible for the effectiveness of DBT cannot be determined with certainty based on current evidence, it is worth noting that the importance of acceptance is a recurring theme in the literature on the psychotherapy of suicide risk. In her book, *Waking Up*, Terry Wise describes her psychotherapy before and after a near lethal suicide attempt. She describes the progression of "…making the unendurable, manageable…" (2012). In his book, *Autopsy of a Suicidal Mind*, the father of suicidology, Edwin Shneidman (2004) described how he would have approached working with a patient who had died by suicide, and whose mother had come to Shneidman trying to find some understanding of her tragic loss. In describing to her how he would have tried to work with her son if he had had the opportunity, Shneidman stated,

> Together, he and I would redefine and fine-tune our understanding that, in actual practice, "unbearable" and "intolerable" really mean barely bearable and somehow tolerable. ... Hopefully, he could come to do what Emperor Hirohito ordered his overwhelmed people to do at the end of World War II: to suffer the insufferable and to endure the unendurable – and to live. (p. 163).

DBT requires constantly balancing validation and problem solving. Validation, the empathetic valuing and support for the patient's own experience, is a core component for any therapeutic relationship, and is likely to be particularly important in working with those who are suicidal. However, validation, as critical as it is, needs to be balanced with helping patients solve the problems that are making them suicidal in the first place. Linehan emphasizes that prolonged focus on either validation or problem solving is unlikely to be effective (1993). The therapist must be attuned enough to the patient's needs and observant enough of the patient's response to therapeutic interventions to be able to know when each is necessary.

Regarding specific mechanisms of change, while cognitive behavior therapy or DBT may place greater emphasis on either changing cognition or regulating emotion as the driving engine for behavior change, these differing emphases are relatively subtle, as cognition, emotion, and behavior are all clearly in a dynamic interplay in each model of treatment.

The findings of the Fleischmann and colleagues (2008) study showing a reduction in deaths by suicide utilizing a combination of an ED intervention and post ED follow-up, when considered in conjunction with the findings of Motto (1976) and Carter and colleagues (2005), suggest that sustained, supportive follow-up contact may also play a key role.

4.6 Efficacy and Prognosis

Several randomized controlled trials (RCTs) of DBT have demonstrated the treatment's effectiveness. The initial study found DBT to be more effective than treatment-as-usual (TAU) in treatment of suicidal patients who met diagnostic criteria for borderline personality disorder (Allmon et al., 1991). Those receiving DBT, compared to TAU, were significantly less likely to engage in suicide attempts or self-harm, and when they did engage in suicidal behaviors, undertook less medically severe acts. Those receiving DBT were also less likely to be hospitalized, had fewer days in hospital, and had higher scores on global and social adjustment. In a second RCT focusing on treatment of women with borderline personality disorder and comorbid substance abuse, Linehan and colleagues (1999) replicated the original study and also found that DBT was more effective than TAU at reducing drug abuse. Koons and colleagues (2001) randomly assigned women veterans diagnosed with borderline personality disorder to either DBT or TAU. Unlike the original studies of Linehan and colleagues (Allmon et al., 1991; Linehan, 1993), subjects were not required to have a recent history of suicidal behavior. Those receiving DBT showed significant reductions in suicidal ideation, depression, hopelessness, and anger compared to TAU. DBT has even shown in an RCT to be superior to an "expert treatment" control condition (Linehan et al., 2006). Efficacy with largely male populations of chronically suicidal patients requires further validation.

An RCT by Brown and colleagues (2005) also demonstrated a reduction in suicide attempts by utilizing a 10-session cognitive therapy intervention with adults who had recently attempted suicide. Participants in the cognitive therapy group were 50% less likely to reattempt than those in the usual care group. Similarly, the RCT by Slee and colleagues (2008) found reductions in reoccurrence of suicidal behavior in a group of 15–35-year-olds who had recently engaged in either a suicide attempt or an episode of self-harm without suicidal intent.

The research by Rudd and Jobes and the recent research on the Attempted Suicide Short Intervention Program (ASSIP) has further established the efficacy of psychotherapeutic treatments for suicidal people. These represent very significant advances with great potential to reduce suicide attempts if they can be widely disseminated. Unfortunately, much less is known about the longer term prognosis for those who attempt suicide or have experienced a suicidal crisis. We do know, thankfully, that most will not go on to die by suicide. We also know that many have provided tremendous inspiration by telling their stories of hope and recovery. But we do not know how many recover completely and thrive vs. those who live lives of "quiet desperation." Nor do we know how our treatments impact these trajectories in the long term although we do know these treatments reduce repeat suicide attempts in the short term. The absence of studies that monitor mortality over time is a particular problem. One encouraging long-term study from Denmark (Erlangsen et al., 2015) did show that referral to suicide prevention centers, which had therapists experienced in working with suicidal patients, saved lives and improved psychosocial outcomes over an approximate 20-year period.

Clinicians must be prepared for the recurrence of suicidality

Since there is not yet evidence based on RCTs that these treatments, promising as they are in reducing suicide attempts, will also prevent deaths by suicide, it is prudent to plan with the patient for the potential recurrence of suicidality. Booster sessions are one reasonable way to do this, although not yet the subject of significant research. The significant evidence showing the effectiveness of nondemanding letters or postcards (Carter et al., 2005; Motto & Bostrum, 2001) suggests that this simple, low-cost intervention be incorporated into clinical practice, and the results of the study by Fleischmann and colleagues (2008) showing a reduction in deaths by suicide using an ED intervention plus follow-up model strongly supports the incorporation of such follow-up activities into all treatments for suicidal patients.

4.7 Variations and Combinations of Methods

4.7.1 The Zero Suicide Model

Significant interest both within the United States and internationally has been generated by an approach to reducing suicide among those receiving healthcare called *zero suicide*. Zero suicide was inspired by the experience of the Henry Ford Health System in reducing suicide by over 60% among those receiving care. The Henry Ford program, originally called perfect depression care, had as a core principle the aspirational goal of zero suicide, i.e., that health and mental health programs should actively strive to not have any suicides among persons under care by systematically using evidence-based care. While on the surface it might seem that all treatment programs strive to not have any suicides, pessimism and fatalism about preventing suicide has led to the absence of strong, systemic efforts utilizing the increase in evidence-based approaches previously reviewed. Some of the core elements of Zero Suicide include systematic screening and risk assessment, establishing protocols for care for those found to be at high risk including the use of collaborative safety planning, the use of evidence-based treatments, careful attention to continuity of care, continuous quality improvement, incorporating the voices of those with lived experience of suicidal crisis or suicide loss, and assuring that providers have been trained in suicide prevention. Yet the experience in some other countries shows that the experience of Henry Ford Health System was not unique. In England, implementation of recommendations from the National Confidential Inquiry into Suicide and Homicide were shown to significantly reduce suicide among those receiving mental healthcare. Of equal importance was the demonstration that this could be done across the country. Similarly, efforts in Denmark have achieved important reductions.

4.7.2 Medication and Psychotherapy

Psychotherapy and pharmacotherapy are frequently used in combination when treating suicidal patients. One advantage of using both in combination is that this typically involves two different providers and it is wise to utilize a team approach when working with high-risk suicidal patients so that ongoing consultation can occur.

Three types of medication are available: lithium, clozaril, and SSRIs

As previously noted, there is research currently regarding the utility of at least three different types of medication. For two of them, lithium with bipolar patients and clozaril with schizophrenia, there is some evidence of effectiveness, although the lithium research does not include a full scale, prospective RCT, and the research on clozaril showed an impact on suicide behavior generally, rather than on deaths by suicide specifically.

For the third type of medication, there has been a firestorm of controversy regarding the use of SSRIs, particularly among youths. The controversy is regarding whether SSRIs might increase the risk of suicide among youths or whether they decrease suicide risk. SSRIs are commonly used in the treatment of depression; indeed, they have been one of the most frequently prescribed medications in the US.

One complexity in any analysis of the relationship between SSRIs and suicidality is that SSRIs are used with many youths (and adults) who are at risk for suicide. It is therefore unclear if reports of suicidality following the onset of treatment result from the underlying disorder or are side effects of the medication.

The controversy over the possible role of SSRIs came to prominence first in England, where the British drug regulating agency ruled that paroxetine (Paxil) should not be used by English physicians for treatment of youths because of evidence of suicidality without evidence of effectiveness to outweigh potential risks. The ruling did not include fluoxetine (Prozac) because studies did exist showing effectiveness for treatment of depression among youths. Much of this work was based on reanalysis of the pharmaceutical industries' original data. There were no completed suicides in the data set but some evidence of increased suicidal ideation or behavior. In the wake of the British decision, in the US, the FDA convened a series of hearings with much anecdotal testimony from people believing SSRIs caused suicides of a loved one. In the FDA analysis, for every 100 youth who received placebo, two became suicidal, but for those treated with SSRIs four out of every 100 became suicidal (US Food & Drug Administration, 2018). Ultimately, the FDA issued a black box warning on the prescription of SSRIs to youths (excluding Prozac). The black box warning emphasized what should have been standard practice in treating persons at risk for suicide: careful monitoring. As a result, the prescription rates of SSRIs have decreased. Some have argued that the decrease in SSRI prescriptions has led to an increase in youth suicide (Gibbons et al., 2007a).

It is important to remember that the black box warning does not recommend against the use of SSRIs, but instead calls for the careful monitoring for suicidality in the days and weeks following the start of antidepressant treatment, the kind of careful monitoring that should be routine when treating all patients at risk for suicide. The availability of medication as a potential treatment modality for those at risk for suicide should be routinely reviewed at the start of treatment as part of an informed consent for treatment, with referral available to a psychiatrist or other health professional skilled in psychopharmacology who can discuss with the patient in detail the potential benefits and risks.

The availability of medication as potential treatment should be reviewed at the start of treatment

4.7.3 Working With Families

The issue of the appropriate role of individual and family interventions is of particular importance in working with those at risk for suicide. Busch and colleagues (2003) have emphasized the importance of health professionals communicating and coordinating with family, as frequently patients hospitalized for suicide risk may not tell a clinician they are thinking about suicide but may have said something to family members that warrants having concern. Similar findings by Barnes and colleagues (2001) with near lethal suicide attempters underscore the importance of working with families. The American Association of Suicidology has published the *AAS Recommendations for Inpatient and Residential Patients Known to be at Elevated Risk for Suicide* which contains numerous recommendations relevant to working with families in inpatient and residential settings (see Box 10). These recommendations, however, are equally applicable to high-risk patients in outpatient settings. They strongly encourage the incorporation of families as meaningful members of the treatment team.

Box 10
Excerpted AAS Family-Focused Recommendations

A) The availability of the family and other sources of support should be assessed, as well as their willingness and ability to provide such support.

B) A family session should routinely be recommended.

C) Both the patient and the family or significant others should be given instruction regarding suicide and its associated risk, including, but not limited to, the following: warning signs of suicide, the increased risk for suicide during hospital passes or following discharge; the need for medication and other treatment adherence; explanation of how psychiatric symptoms may impair judgment; explanation of the need for the patient to avoid use of intoxicants and how intoxicants increase risk; the need for the removal of the means for suicide, and the particular risk associated with firearms.

D) The patient and family or significant others should be given explicit instructions on how to access the treating physician or therapist regarding questions, observations, or concerns, and should be given information regarding how to access treating clinicians after office hours and any limitations on their availability. Emergency phone numbers that are available 24 hours a day, 7 days a week, such as psychiatric emergency services and crisis lines, should also be given.

E) If family members or significant others are asked to assist in the outpatient monitoring of risk, specific instructions should be given, including action steps to be taken in the event of felt concern or the development of a crisis. Consideration should be given to providing these in writing, as oral instructions may be difficult to recall accurately in the midst of a crisis.

F) Where permitted by law, and with the patient's written permission, the patient's family members or significant others should be alerted to the patient's history of suicidal thinking, feeling, behavior, and nonfatal suicide attempts.

Adapted from the American Association of Suicidology, 2008

Families should be routinely involved in the treatment of suicidal persons, unless there is a specific contraindication

There are many reasons to involve the family and/or significant others routinely in the care of suicidal persons. Too often, clinicians involve families only when they see a specific indication. Rather than needing a specific indication, families should be involved in the treatment of suicidal persons routinely, and only not involved if there is a specific contraindication, such as abuse.

4.7.4 Treatment of Adolescents

There are numerous compelling reasons why the treatment of suicidal adolescents is of great importance. Most obviously, the death of a child or teenager by suicide is an immense tragedy, a preventable loss of a person whose whole life was in front of them. However, since the ratio of suicidal ideation or attempts to suicide deaths among adolescents is much greater among youth, that is, suicidal youth are less likely to die by suicide than those in midlife or older, there is a tendency to take a youth's suicidal thoughts or behavior less seriously than that of an older person. This is a major mistake. Not only is it important that there always be vigilance regarding the possibility of a suicide death, the importance of suicidality in a youth as a marker for future psychiatric comorbidity must also be recognized.

In a longitudinal study of youth with suicidal thoughts and behaviors, these thoughts and behaviors were found to be a marker for a multitude of poor psychiatric and functional outcomes in adulthood (Copeland et al., 2017). While some of this association was accounted for by shared association of suicidal thoughts and behavior in youth with depression and anxiety, there was also a strong independent relationship with adult suicidal thoughts and behaviors. In addition, outcomes for children who had suicidal ideation alone were just as negative as those with suicide attempts, particularly if the suicidal ideation was combined with depression. One in two youth with suicidal thoughts and depression went on to have suicidal ideation or attempts as adults while for youth who had suicidal ideation without depression the likelihood of suicidal ideation or attempts as adults was one in ten (Copeland et al., 2017). Given this, the importance of early detection and effective treatment of suicidal youth becomes paramount. In the United States, youth suicide prevention programs that focused on early identification followed by effective treatment were associated in a national study with decreased youth suicide rates as well as decreased suicide attempts (Garraza et al., 2019).

One in two youth with suicidal thoughts and depression went on to have suicidal ideation or attempts as adults

As with treatments for many problems, treatments developed for adults cannot be assumed to be applicable to adolescents without adaptation. A version of DBT has been developed for adolescents (Miller et al., 2007). Using a quasi-experimental design, adolescent DBT was found to reduce suicidal ideation, reduce rates of psychiatric hospitalization, and increase treatment completion when compared to treatment as usual. The adolescent DBT model involves the family in skills training, and, like DBT for adults, includes both a group and an individual component. More recently, in a randomized controlled trial in Norway, the adolescent DBT program was found to reduce episodes of self-harm as well as suicidal ideation and depression in outpatients with recent and repetitive self-harm (Mehlum et al., 2014) In addition to dialectical behavior therapy for adolescents, other adolescent therapies with evidence of effectiveness include safe alternatives for teens and youth (Asarnow et al., 2015), and attachment based family therapy (Diamond et al., 2010). Of particular interest is the work of Cheryl King with youth nominated support teams, which has shown preliminary evidence of decreased mortality over a 10–14-year time frame, the only treatment for suicidal adolescents to do so (King et al., 2019).

Family involvement is of particular importance in the treatment of adolescents at risk for suicide. Communication about the level of suicide risk to parents is extremely important along with the plan for addressing that risk and instructions for how to respond to escalations in suicidality. In some states there are legal requirements for such disclosures. As pointed out by Berman and colleagues (2006), suicidal adolescents in treatment rarely self-refer. Most often, they are brought to treatment by parents or guardians. Therefore, engaging families and keeping them involved and informed is essential for suc-

Family involvement is of particular importance in the treatment of adolescents

cessful treatment to take place. Even if individual psychotherapy is the major intervention utilized, family intervention will need to take place as well. It is important to remember that having a family member who is thinking about suicide can be intensely anxiety provoking and the response to such anxiety can range from denial, to anger, to overwhelming worry and the need to constantly be checking on the adolescent's state of mind and emotional health. Therapy can be extremely important for helping families to find ways to cope with the understandable anxiety inherent in this situation.

Children and teens who attended a follow-up appointment within 1 week of being discharged from a psychiatric hospital were half as likely to die by suicide over the next six months

The crucial importance of hospitalized adolescents receiving rapid post-discharge follow-up was demonstrated in a recent important study. Children and teens who attended a follow-up appointment within 1 week of being discharged from a psychiatric hospital were half as likely to die by suicide over the next 6 months compared with similarly hospitalized youth who did not attend a mental health appointment, a retrospective, longitudinal cohort study found (Fontanella et al., 2020).

There is evidence that a group at particularly high risk for suicidal behavior, particularly suicide attempts, is adolescents who are gay, lesbian bisexual, or transgendered (D'Augelli et al., 2005). A particular high-risk time may be the period when a youth discloses their sexual orientation to their family. Family support and connectedness appears to be particularly important in protection against suicide attempts (Eisenberg & Resnick, 2006). Rates of attempted suicide by LGBT young people whose parents tried to change their sexual orientation were more than double (48%) the rate of LGBT young adults who reported no conversion experiences (22%). *Suicide attempts nearly tripled for LGBT young people who reported both home-based efforts to change their sexual orientation by parents* ***and*** *intervention efforts by therapists and religious leaders (63%).* Therapy therefore needs to focus on family acceptance.

An additional group of youth at high risk for death by suicide and suicide attempts is American Indian and Alaska Native youth. Using a comprehensive approach that included as a cornerstone outreach in their homes with any youth identified with suicidal thoughts or an attempt through a tribally mandated surveillance system, suicidal behavior was reduced by almost 40% (Cwik et al., 2016).

4.7.5 Individual and Group Treatment

For many years clinical lore advised against the use of group modalities with those who had attempted suicide or were otherwise at risk for suicide. Fear of patients inadvertently harming each other through sharing the details of their suicide attempts was likely a part of this fear. However, the success of DBT in combining individual and group treatment has convincingly demonstrated that the addition of group modalities can be potentially of great value. In DBT, the group focus is on skills training and the fears regarding contagion or negative influences are dealt with by providing the skills training with clear guidelines on maintaining the focus on the teaching of skills, with suicidal communications dealt with by rapid referral to the individual therapist upon the ending of the group.

Also noteworthy is an increasing focus in recent years on peer support services. Peer support groups and other peer support services exist for those struggling with mental illness. Those that focus on suicide attempt survivors and others at risk for suicide have been growing but are not yet widely available, nor have they as yet been rigorously evaluated. However, given the demonstrated difficulties in engaging those at risk for suicide in formal mental services, peer support services hold great promise. A manual for a support group for suicide attempt survivors has been created by the Didi Hirsch Mental Health Services Suicide Prevention Center (2014) and is now being used in multiple settings.

4.8 Problems in Carrying Out the Treatments

4.8.1 Problems in Communication and Information Gathering

In a unique project sponsored by the American Foundation for Suicide Prevention, a registry of 36 patients who died by suicide while in treatment was created utilizing questionnaires and case narratives submitted by therapists who had lost a patient to suicide and were willing to share information about the treatment (Hendin et al., 2006). While the findings from this study may not be representative of all patients who died by suicide while in treatment, the results are nonetheless instructive. One pattern was the lack of active communication among all treatment providers involved in the care of the patients. Although 23 patients had been in treatment with another provider previously, communication between the current and previous therapist was described as rare (Hendin et al., 2006). In four instances, there was lack of communication between a therapist and a psychiatrist who were treating the patient together. Such lack of communication prevents the sharing of potentially critical information. While it is unclear if the frequency of consultation with past treatment providers and the obtaining of prior records among this sample is any worse than in common clinical practice, it is clear that obtaining such information is particularly important when treating high-risk patients. Similarly, consultation with other providers is widely regarded as part of the standard of care for treating suicidal patients (Bongar, 2002). Consultation provides support and an additional perspective for therapists facing some of the most difficult clinical decisions they are called upon to make. It is for this reason that Linehan (1993) has built a consultation team into DBT as an essential component of the treatment.

An additional problem in treatment highlighted in the registry was the lack of treatment for substance abuse. In 11 of the 36 cases, obvious substance abuse was never treated (Hendin et al., 2006).

In many suicides, obvious substance abuse was never treated

4.8.2 Problems in Continuity of Care

For all clinicians, losing a patient to suicide is one of the greatest traumas they will encounter in their professional lives. Yet, until recently, very little information was available in the US regarding how often suicide occurred among those receiving mental health treatment. In the UK, the National Confidential Inquiry into Suicide and Homicide by People with Mental Illness (Appleby et al., 2001) found that approximately one quarter of all people who died by suicide in England, Wales, Scotland, and Northern Ireland had been in contact with mental health services in the year before death. Suicide on inpatient units accounted for 10%–16%, depending on the country. An even larger number, 23%–30% died within 3 months of discharge from an inpatient unit, with a peak in the first 2 weeks following discharge. Just under one third of suicides in the community missed their final outpatient sessions. An assertive effort was made to re-establish contact in about half of these cases.

In a population-based analysis of all suicide decedents in Toronto, Canada, 66% had a mental healthcare contact in the year before death with the most common being an outpatient primary care visit (with a psychiatric diagnosis), an outpatient psychiatric visit or an ED visit for a mental health issue (Schaffer et al., 2016) This type of data, so critical for mental health service delivery, has not previously been available in the US on a national level or on a scale as large as a state. Yet this information is critical for guiding suicide prevention efforts, such as enhancing risk assessment capacities, improving continuity of care, and preventing drop out from treatment. However, no large-scale data from the US were available until the publication of data from the National Violent Death Reporting System (NVDRS).

Looking at data across 13 states, Karch and colleagues (2006) found rates of current mental health treatment ranged from 32.8% for white non-Hispanics to 15.2% for Hispanics. Results from Sanford and colleagues (2006) indicated that 58% of females in North Carolina but only 32.5% of males were receiving current mental health treatment.

Similar data were also found in the state of Maryland. Women ages 45–59 years had the highest rate of suicide among all age groups for females and 74% of them were in mental health treatment at the time of their suicide. In contrast, 33% of men in that same age group who died by suicide were in mental health treatment. Powell and colleagues (2006) interpret these results as meaning that improving mental healthcare for women is an indicated suicide prevention strategy, but may be less so for men. In contrast, for men, promoting help seeking might be more important.

Data of particular importance are available from the state of South Carolina, where NVDRS data have been linked to a human resources database to allow precise information to be available regarding the most recent healthcare contact prior to death by suicide. Of 491 suicides that took place in the state during the year 2004, 20 suicides occurred within 7 days of discharge from an ED or inpatient unit, and 27 more died within 30 days of discharge (Weis et al., 2006). This means that in the state of South Carolina, more than 4% of all suicides took place within 7 days of discharge from an acute care setting and almost 10% of all suicides took place within 30 days of discharge from such a setting. Like the findings from the UK, these findings underscore the importance of further research into discharge decision-making, risk assessment protocols, and continuity of care following discharge to help us reduce this tragic toll.

Acute treatments are generally regarded as essential when working with suicidal patients, but such treatments are typically short-term, and while they may lessen suicide risk at times of exceptionally high risk, they are unlikely to eliminate suicide risk entirely. This makes the follow-up to acute care particularly important. The IOM found that those at risk for suicide are "insufficiently followed after acute treatment" (Institute of Medicine et al., 2002). Given this well documented increased risk after inpatient discharge and other acute care discharge, careful follow-up is clearly indicated. Outpatient therapists, who may be used to having weekly psychotherapy sessions with their patients, or outpatient clinics, which may have long waiting lists and demands for therapist's time, should schedule appointments for discharged patients as soon as possible after discharge, within 48 hours if possible, but always within a week. The recent study by Fontanella and colleagues (2020) showed that adolescents discharged from inpatient psychiatric care were half as likely to die by suicide if they were seen within 7 days.

The scientific evidence shows that the immediate period after psychiatric hospitalization and ER discharge of suicidal persons is a time of greatly heightened risk

In recent years, the scientific evidence has become overwhelming that the immediate period after both psychiatric hospitalization and ER discharge of suicidal people is a time of heightened risk, but all too often it is characterized by poor follow-up and limited continuity of care (Goldman-Mellor et al., 2019; Valenstein et al., 2009). The science tells us what we need to do (While et al., 2012) as the evidence that staying in close contact with these patients, collaborating with them on safety plans or crisis response plans, attending to the availability of lethal means and increasing social support, can reduce suicidal behavior and save lives. These should be components of every episode of care for suicidal people.

Follow-up care, safety or crisis support plans, reduction of access to lethal means, and increasing social support should be components of care

4.8.3 Problems in Initial Risk Assessment

Additional information from South Carolina indicated that 18.5% of suicides were receiving outpatient mental health services in the public sector (Weis et al., 2006). No information was available about those who might have been seen in private practice settings. Nine were seen within a week of their suicide, two within 24 hours. Of those being seen in the outpatient public mental health system, the median number of visits was 8, meaning that many of these persons were relatively new to the mental health system. This suggests that many suicides that took place by patients within mental health systems may occur with patients who have not yet established a meaningful therapeutic relationship with a clinician. It may also be that either the initial assessment of suicide risk was incomplete or the relationship was not deep enough for the patient to reveal the depth of their despair or the content of their ideation. This would underline the importance of a thorough, comprehensive suicide risk assessment taking place within the context of a developing, collaborative relationship. The South Carolina data also pointed to the existence of a subgroup of suicide deaths by patients with very large numbers of contacts, possibly pointing to a clustering of multiple suicide attempters.

Many suicides may take place with patients who have not yet established a meaningful therapeutic relationship with a clinician

4.8.4 Problems in Collaboration

A critical issue in the treatment of persons at risk for suicide is whether the patient is able to be a collaborative partner in keeping themselves alive. The combination of high, acute risk and the inability to establish a collaborative relationship is an indication for hospitalization. Breakdowns in collaboration must be addressed as a very high priority. There are times when a clinician will need to act unilaterally to safeguard the patient, making emergency decisions either without the patient's consent or even against the patient's explicit wishes. Intervening with an intoxicated, suicidal patient with access to lethal means would be a clear example.

However, this should always be a last resort. It is imperative that clinicians working with suicidal patients not practice defensive kind of mental health. As Simon (2004) emphasizes, "Good clinical care is always the best risk management." In addition, we have distressingly little empirical data to assist us in determining what the impact of involuntary or coercive interventions are on long-term suicide risk. Interventions that decrease suicide risk in the coming days or weeks (e.g., involuntary hospitalization) may inadvertently increase suicide risk in the future in those cases in which our patients are reluctant to share with us their suicidal thoughts and urges for fear of involuntary intervention. When this occurs, we are less able to assist them in their struggle to stay alive. This may be particularly true for patients whose competence to make decisions is not obviously compromised by intoxication or active psychosis.

Linehan builds into her treatment model a mechanism for continuing to work on collaboration between patient and therapist throughout the treatment. She introduces the concept of therapy interfering behavior (Linehan, 1993), which is anything that patients might do that would make the therapist want to terminate therapy and anything that the therapist might do that would make the patient want to drop out. Therapy interfering behavior is second only to suicidal behavior in the DBT hierarchy of targets in treatment (Linehan, 1993).

Persons at risk for suicide who drop out of treatment should be actively outreached

Drop out and poor follow-up are also issues that need to be addressed. At-risk patients who fail to show up for appointments should be actively outreached. For patients at risk who drop out of treatment, it is recommended that therapists incorporate as a standard part of their treatment protocol for high-risk patients the episodic mailing of nondemanding follow-up letters as per the findings of Motto and Bostrum (2001) and Carter and colleagues (2005). The potential significance of routinely incorporating such a simple intervention, both within systems of care and in private practices, is highlighted by the findings by Gibb and colleagues (2005), who describe the poor attendance rate of the suicide attempt population where only 30%–60% attend follow-up appointments.

4.9 Multicultural Issues

There are important cultural differences in suicide rates, frequency of suicide attempts, and attitudes toward suicide (see Box 11). Despite this, little systematic research attention has been paid to the clinical implications of these differences in suicidal behavior and attitudes toward suicide among the major ethnic and cultural groups in the US (Range et al., 1999). This lack of focus is unfortunate as sociocultural norms can either facilitate or inhibit suicidal behavior (Orbach, 1997). Important questions remain to be answered. For example, why do African American women have one of the lowest suicide rates in the nation? What promotes this level of resilience, what protective factors are present that lead to such low rates despite significant socioeconomic stress and historical trauma? Conversely, what leads rates of suicide to be so high among American Indian youth and why is there such marked tribal variability?

Box 11
Multicultural Disparities in Suicidal Behavior in the US

According to the Centers for Disease Control and Prevention (CDC, 2011), there are marked disparities present regarding suicidal behavior among ethnic and cultural groups. These include:

- Among American Indians/Alaska Natives ages 15–34 years, suicide is the second leading cause of death.
- Suicide rates among American Indian/Alaskan Native adolescents and young adults ages 15–34 years (21.4 per 100,000) are 1.9 times higher than the national average for that age group (11.5 per 100,000).
- Hispanic female high school students in grades 9–12 reported a higher percentage of suicide attempts (14.9%) than their White, non-Hispanic (9.3%) or Black, non-Hispanic (9.8%) counterparts.

An analysis of the risk of suicide among Hispanic females ages 12–17 years conducted during the 2000 National Household Survey on Drug Abuse found they were at heightened risk of suicidal behavior compared to other youths (Substance Abuse and Mental Health Services Administration, 2003). Youths were asked during the interview whether they had thought seriously about killing themselves or tried to kill themselves during the 12 months before the survey interview. In addition, Hispanic females were less likely to have received treatment for their suicidal thoughts or attempts with only 32% having received treatment. And those girls who did receive treatment were less likely than other youths to have had their suicidality be the reason for treatment, making it less likely that even those who received treatment received specific evidence-based treatments focused on their suicide risk.

A byproduct of the early developmental stage of research into suicide and suicide prevention is that, despite the clear prominence of cultural issues in suicide, there is little specific information available about effective treatments for culturally diverse groups.

The lack of research data is particularly prominent among the cultural group with the highest rate of youth suicide in the US: American Indians and Alaska Natives. There is little information available about the efficacy of either DBT or cognitive behavior therapy with either group. The most encouraging results have come from the Western Athabaskan Natural Helpers Program which demonstrated a 61% decrease in suicide attempts among youth during 12 years of implementation (May et al., 2005). This program worked with Natural Helpers, members of the tribal community who provided lay counseling to those identified as being at risk, with therapy by professionals

Death by suicide in the White Mountain Apache tribe was reduced using rapid contact with suicidal youth as well as interventions based on Apache culture

reserved for those assessed at more serious risk. Also encouraging was the finding in the White Mountain Apache tribe that suicide could be reduced using a combination of universal, selected, and indicated prevention strategies with the core intervention being the ability to rapidly make contact and follow any tribal youth who is known to be thinking about suicide or who has made a suicide attempt (Cwik et al, 2016). Less information is available about culturally specific therapeutic interventions.

Rotheram-Borus and colleagues (2000) studied an ED intervention with Latina females. Young female suicide attempters and their families were interviewed in the ER, shown a psychoeducational videotape, and encouraged to enroll in outpatient psychotherapy. Those who received the intervention were more likely to follow-up in treatment. The intervention also incorporated training of ED staff.

Kaslow and colleagues (2002) studied risk for suicidal behavior among low-income African American women and found that risk factors include physical and nonphysical partner abuse, childhood maltreatment, posttraumatic stress, hopelessness, psychological distress, and drug abuse. These findings underline the importance, both in outpatient and emergency settings, of screening for both suicide risk and domestic violence, whenever one of them is present.

The recent increase in suicide in the United States among very young black children (Bridge et al., 2015) underscores the need both to better understand what is driving the increase in suicide among black children ages 5–11 years as well as to develop approaches for successful intervention. Deepening our understanding of the cultural context of suicide and of the effectiveness of culturally congruent interventions is a crucial priority for the field of suicide prevention.

5

Case Vignette

Julie

This is a brief case study of a 28-year-old Greek American woman with several suicide attempts. She entered outpatient treatment at a community mental health center following a psychiatric hospitalization for one of these attempts. Because of her history of prior suicide attempts as well as frequent suicidal ideation, she was referred for admission to the dialectical behavior therapy (DBT) treatment program. Her inpatient clinician had obtained the client's permission to both contact this clinician and forward her inpatient records. During the consultation with her inpatient clinician, her suicidal history, precipitants for self-destructive actions, suicide risk factors, and diagnostic and treatment history were reviewed.

At the initial session, with the therapist's encouragement, Julie described the pain that she has been experiencing that led to her suicidal behavior. The therapist encouraged her to tell her story, weaving into their conversations questions designed to help him understand how she had come to the brink of self-destruction and to obtain the information necessary for a comprehensive risk assessment. Julie was experiencing significant psychosocial stress, including being unable to continue to work at a professional position at which she had previously excelled. She also was estranged from most members of her family. She experienced intense negative emotions in response to these stressors, including most prominently anxiety, guilt, and shame. In addition to these major stressors, she also responded with great emotional intensity to the stresses and strains of daily life. These emotions would frequently propel self-destructive behavior, including episodes of self-cutting. These episodes were frequently accompanied by suicidal ideation.

Julie was oriented to DBT. Like many patients she responded positively to being told that her emotional sensitivity was not under her cognitive control, and was something she needed to learn to accept and cope with, rather than suppress and castigate herself for. She was relieved to learn that her sensitivity was not her fault, but worried that she had to learn to better tolerate and regulate her emotions without resorting to suicidal behavior. She agreed to accept as a goal of treatment that she would work to keep herself alive, no matter what, during the 1-year treatment commitment to DBT. She agreed to attend both weekly individual therapy and a weekly DBT skills training group. She worked with the therapist on a safety plan, which included calling the therapist prior to engaging in suicidal behavior and calling the psychiatric emergency service if the therapist was not available. When it emerged during the interview that the patient carried razor blades in her purse "in case I need them," she agreed to give them to the therapist. Julie would not allow her family to be contacted but did agree to have a close friend, who lived nearby, be called.

At the beginning of treatment Julie was cutting herself several times per week. She struggled to remain in the DBT skills training group for the entire session. She would be able to remain in the group when skills were being taught, but when it was her turn to report on how she had used the skills in the past week, she would experience a flood of panic and flee from the group. Then, ashamed of how she reacted and fearful of how her therapist would respond, she would experience suicidal ideation and cut herself.

There were also episodes in which her cutting was not limited to a single cut but where she would make multiple cuts or would have multiple episodes of cutting within a period of hours. The therapist closely consulted with Julie's psychiatrist and on two occasions where her cutting escalated (one of which culminated in an overdose), she was hospitalized.

Following each episode of self-harm, Julie and the therapist would conduct a behavioral chain analysis, a detailed examination of the flow of events, thoughts, emotions, and behaviors leading to the episode. The functional relationship among these would be explored. For example, her cutting and overdosing functioned as escape behavior. They distracted Julie from her surging dysphoric emotions, reducing the pain. The self- destructive behavior was being negatively reinforced by the momentary pain reduction. Even her suicidal ideation functioned as a distractor from her intense emotions. In fact, suicidal thoughts appeared to be an automatic response to negative emotions. On her diary cards, which she filled out daily, suicidal ideation was found to be present every day, although the frequency and intensity varied from day to day. Because of the daily experience of suicidal thoughts, suicidal ideation alone was not considered an indication for hospitalization.

Single episodes of cutting, even when accompanied by suicidal ideation, were also not considered indications for hospitalization.

Hospitalization was an aversive experience for Julie who experienced a deep sense of failure with each hospital admission. Psychiatric admissions also tended to reinforce her view of herself as crazy and incompetent and decreased her sense of self-efficacy in being able to cope with her own emotions. Psychiatric hospitalizations were thus used sparingly with Julie and only when necessary to interrupt an escalating series of self-destructive behaviors.

Treatment focused on helping Julie learn how to cope with intense negative emotions without resorting to self-destructive behavior. Expressions of suicidality were found to be triggered by intolerable thoughts and emotions. Identifying these emotions and encouraging Julie to sit for a moment with these feelings utilizing mindfulness skills was a major focus of therapy during individual sessions. Julie and her therapist were able to identify that strong emotions, particularly sadness and shame, triggered panic and anxiety which in turn triggered a tremendous urge to escape. By helping Julie to focus her attention on the feelings that she usually fled from, Julie gradually learned that these feelings could be tolerated. This constituted a form of exposure therapy. The therapist was able to provide immediate support to Julie as she sat with these feelings.

Outside of sessions an emphasis was placed on the distress tolerance skills taught in the skills training group. These crisis survival strategies included distraction techniques, including holding an ice cube and focusing all of her attention on the cold sensations. Further analysis of her reaction to many interpersonal situations, including being in the DBT skills training group, revealed that when she was flooded with panic, she would feel that she couldn't breathe unless she escaped the situation. Cognitive behavior techniques for the treatment of anxiety disorders, such as diaphragmatic breathing, were incorporated into the treatment to help her manage her anxiety.

While Julie continued to experience suicidal thoughts on a daily basis, the frequency of cutting, overdosing, and psychiatric hospitalizations gradually decreased. When episodes of cutting did occur, they tended to be associated with efforts to return to work. Julie made several such attempts. These efforts invariably increased the amount of anxiety and panic she experienced and the likelihood of suicidal behavior if she did not succeed in coping with the job demands. On several occasions she had to leave work due to the anxiety, leading to an escalating suicidal crisis. The behavioral principle of shaping was used to help Julie look for work that did not have intensive social or interpersonal demands, to heighten the likelihood that she could keep the job and lessen the likelihood of self-destructive behavior.

The telephone was used extensively to help coach Julie through crisis periods without resorting to self- destructive behavior. Typically, if Julie could reach her therapist, he could walk her through the skills she had been taught and cutting or overdosing could be averted. If the therapist could not be reached, Julie had, as part of her safety plan, the phone number for the mental health center's psychiatric emergency service. Julie's response to psychiatric emergency service intervention in the first few months of treatment was quite varied as she was extremely sensitive to being a "burden" to the system and would tend to react to even subtle cues that she was taking too much time or that the emergency clinician had other people to respond to, by apologizing, getting off the phone, and cutting herself.

In order to help Julie deal with the emergency service more effectively, the therapist assisted Julie in writing out instructions for the emergency service regarding what she would find most useful in getting her through a crisis. This plan was then placed in the emergency service's "at risk" file which was reviewed by emergency clinicians at the start of each shift.

By the end of one year of DBT Julie was able to regularly attend skills group and while the frequency of self- destructive episodes and psychiatric hospitalization were clearly decreased, persistent suicidal ideation and occasional episodes of self-harm remained. Julie, her therapist, and her psychiatrist decided she would remain in DBT until self-destructive behavior could be eliminated. Ultimately, for Julie, the goal is not simply the absence of self-destructive behavior but rather achieving a life that she feels is worth living.

6

Case Example

Intake Evaluation and Treatment Plan

Identifying Data:

Dana is a 17-year-old, Caucasian female who was referred by her mother who accompanied her to the intake evaluation. This is her first application for outpatient treatment.

Chief Complaint:

Her boyfriend's suicide.

History of Present Problem:

Two weeks ago, the patient's boyfriend died by suicide. She had been unaware of any prior suicidal thinking on his part. At the time that he killed himself, she had just been on the telephone with him.

They had had a disagreement earlier, but had just resolved it. She had asked to speak to a mutual friend who was at the boyfriend's house at the time. While the patient and the friend were on the telephone, there was a noise and the friend told the patient that the boyfriend had shot himself, and told her to get help. She did not believe him at first. When the friend put the phone next to her boyfriend, she heard a low moaning sound. She then hung up in a panic and called the police who went to the house. She did not hear anything for a few hours and then was informed that her boyfriend was dead. The patient has internalized blame for this tragedy and feels that he killed himself because of her. This is because she had been told by the friend that her boyfriend had made a statement shortly before the phone call, referring to her and saying "I love her too much. I can't take it." She also felt guilty that she did not believe that he had shot himself, and did not immediately call for help.

However, she remains extremely confused as she is unable to recall anything from the telephone conversation itself that would seem to even hint at suicide. For this reason, she wonders whether it could have been an accident, or even whether the friend may have shot him. (There are apparently rumors to this effect circulating at the local high school.)

In the days following the death, Dana was mostly at home alone with her sister. Her parents were at a retreat. They were in telephone contact with Dana and asked her if she needed them to come home but she told them no. However, she later acknowledged to them, and to this clinician, that she was having suicidal ideation. Dana felt that her boyfriend wanted her to join him.

She had thought about carbon monoxide poisoning and about cutting her wrists, and finally developed a plan where she would take an overdose of Prozac, which had been prescribed for her by her family physician to help her through the bereavement. The day she picked for the suicide attempt was 1 week prior to this appointment and one day before her parents returned from their retreat. She states that she had the bottle of pills in front of her and wrote a suicide note. But then she began to think about what her parents would go through if she killed herself. She also thought that at least now she had memories of her boyfriend and if she killed herself, she didn't know whether she would still have those memories. Finally, she was also afraid that if she took the overdose she might end up as a vegetable. She ultimately aborted the attempt by deciding that if her boyfriend really wanted her to join him, then he would find a way to tell her. She didn't really feel that he would be likely to somehow materialize and so in an important sense this was a way of deciding not to die by suicide. However, she does experience him as being close by and she talks to him frequently. After her parents arrived home, she told them that she had thought of suicide, and they made arrangements for this appointment. Since that time, she has continued to have suicidal thoughts, though she reports these thoughts are weaker and less frequent than previously and are easier to distract herself from. She reports that she has not had any thoughts about suicide today. When asked if talking about her boyfriend's death in the therapy session made her think about suicide, she said no.

Past Psychiatric History:
Dana has no past episodes of psychiatric illness. There also does not appear to be any past history of drug or alcohol abuse. There is no family history of depression or suicide, although there was an uncle who had some kind of emotional disturbance, the nature of which is unknown at present.

Mental Status:
Dana was oriented to person, place, and time. She exhibited no unusual motor behaviors. Her long- and short- term memory seemed intact. Intelligence was judged to be at least average. Judgment and insight seemed good. Mood appeared to be depressed as would be expected in someone recently bereaved. She admitted to occasional suicidal ideation, but no homicidal ideation. Thought processes were logical and coherent. There was no evidence of any thought disorder or delusional thinking. She denied auditory or visual hallucinations.

Assessment:
F43.21 Adjustment Disorder with depressed mood: complicated grieving
Dana presents with depressed mood and suicidal ideation which clearly had its onset at the time of her boyfriend's suicide. What would probably best capture the essence of Dana's clinical condition at this time is to consider this a bereavement that is complicated because of the presence of suicidal ideation. The death of a loved one through suicide often results in a complicated bereavement with a wide range of intense emotional responses and in this instance her reaction is intensified by the fact that she had been on the telephone with him at the time he died by suicide.

In evaluating Dana's level of suicidal risk, several factors are important. She has no past history of suicide attempts or of suicidal ideation. There is no family history of suicide. She is not drug or alcohol involved. She did have both suicidal intent and a suicide plan approximately 1 week ago. The presence of suicide intent was indicated by her writing a suicide note and she made preparations for a suicide attempt by placing the medication in front of her that she was going to use in an overdose. The potential lethality of the aborted attempt was mild to moderate. A factor lessening the extent of suicidal risk is that at the moment when her suicidal intent was the greatest, during the initial overwhelming feelings of shock and distress, Dana was able to cognitively work through and evaluate the advantages of living over dying, and was able to choose life. Another positive sign is that since that time, while there has remained some episodic suicidal ideation, it has been lessening and has been without intent or clear plan. Additionally, it appears clear that Dana's suicidal ideation is intricately linked with her coming to terms with the reality of the loss of her boyfriend. She wants to kill herself only so she could join him, and if this reunion fantasy were not possible, she states she would not want to kill herself. This suggests that through therapy she would come more to terms with the reality of this loss, and would then give less consideration to her self-described "fantasy" of joining him. It is significant that at this point in time she states that she would only kill herself if her boyfriend literally appeared to her and told her to kill herself so she could join him. Since the patient is not at all psychotic and she is well aware that this would not happen, and since she specifically denies that she would act on such ideation if he, for example, appeared to her in a dream, the overall level of suicidal risk at this moment appears low.

Treatment Plan:

Goal 1: Suicidal ideation: The goal will be the elimination of all suicidal ideation within a 2-month time frame. The means for attaining this goal were discussed with the patient and with her mother. Hospitalization was included in the review of treatment alternatives as the safest option. Since her present level of suicidal risk did not seem high, both Dana and her mother felt that she did not need hospitalization and would prefer instead an outpatient treatment option. Outpatient psychotherapy seems to be a feasible alternative considering the overall low level of suicidal risk currently, and that the patient and mother understand the benefits and risk of outpatient therapy compared to hospitalization. Given that Dana was still experiencing some episodic suicidal ideation, another appointment was made for later in the week. Weekly sessions were to follow afterwards. Dana and her mother were given the telephone number for the psychiatric emergency service and Dana was able to clearly state that she would call before acting on any suicidal ideation. Dana's mother agreed that she would lock up all medication in the house. Both Dana and her mother reported that there were no firearms in the house. Consultation was obtained with the staff psychiatrist who concurred with the plan.

Goal 2: Complicated bereavement: While it is hoped that Dana will be completely free of suicidal ideation within 2 months with weekly psychotherapy sessions, it is unlikely that this would be sufficient to help her work through completely the complexity of her bereavement. Indicators of improvement will be when she ceases to blame herself for her boyfriend's suicide, when the ruminative preoccupation with his death decreases substantially (i.e., decrease of 75% of such statements), and when she is able to invest her energies again in age appropriate social and dating activities. The time frame for achieving these goals would be 4 months with weekly psychotherapy sessions.

7

Further Reading

American Psychiatric Association. (2003). *Practice guideline for the assessment and treatment of patients with suicidal behavior*.
The only currently existing set of professional guidelines for assessing and treating suicidal patients.

Berman, A., Jobes, D., & Silverman, M. (2006). *Adolescent suicide: Assessment and intervention.* American Psychological Association.
Widely regarded as the most authoritative text on the assessment, management, and treatment of adolescents at risk for suicide. A comprehensive and empirically based review.

Bongar, B. (2002). *The suicidal patient: Clinical and legal standards of care*. American Psychological Association. https://doi.org/10.1037/10424-000
The definitive source on standards of care in treating suicidal patients.

Bryan, C., & Rudd, D. (2018). *Brief cognitive behavioral therapy for suicide prevention.* Guilford Press.
Treatment manual for innovative brief therapy with strong evidence in clinical trials including crisis response planning.

Jobes, D. (2006). *Managing suicidal risk: A collaborative approach*. Guilford Press.
Treatment manual for the Collaborative Assessment and Management of Suicidality Project. Useful for a wide range of mental health professionals regardless of theoretical orientation.

Joiner, T. (2005). *Why people die by suicide*. Harvard University Press.
A masterful integration of the research on why people die by suicide, leading to a potentially groundbreaking conceptualization of the central roles of suicidal desire and suicidal capacity.

Knapp, S. J. (2020). *Suicide prevention: An ethically and scientifically informed approach.* American Psychological Association. https://doi.org/10.1037/0000145-000
This book targets therapists who work with suicidal adults, with a particular emphasis on the ethical issues involved in working with suicidal patients.

Linehan, M. M. (1993). *Cognitive behavioral treatment of borderline personality disorder.* Guilford Press.
Comprehensive treatment manual for dialectical behavior therapy. The most thorough, science-based resource currently available for treating chronically suicidal patients with borderline personality disorder.

Michel, K., & Gysin-Mailart, A., (2015). *ASSIP: Attempted Suicide Short Intervention Program.* Hogrefe Publishing.
A complete treatment manual that describes an innovative and effective brief therapy program for suicidal patients.

Rudd, M. D., Joiner, T., & Rahab, M. H. (2001). *Treating suicidal behavior: An effective time limited approach*. Guilford Press.
Empirically supported treatment manual for time-limited psychotherapeutic treatment of suicidal behavior.

Shea, S. (2002). *The practical art of suicide assessment: A guide for mental health professionals and substance abuse counselors*. John Wiley.
A major contribution to the art and science of suicide risk assessment.

Shneidman, E. S. (1996). *The suicidal mind.* Oxford University Press.
A concise introduction to the contributions of the founder of the first suicide prevention programs in the United States.

8

References

Allmon, D., Armstrong, H. E., Heard, H. L., Linehan, M. M., & Suarez, A. (1991). Cognitive-behavioral treatment of chronically parasuicidal borderline patients. *Archives of General Psychiatry, 48*(12), 1060–1064. https://doi.org/10.1001/archpsyc.1991.01810360024003

American Association of Suicidology. (2008). *AAS recommendations for inpatient and residential patients known to be at elevated risk for suicide*.

American Foundation for Suicide Prevention. (2016). *State laws on suicide prevention training for health professionals*. https://www.afsp.org

American Psychiatric Association. (2013). *Diagnostic and statistical manual of mental disorders,* 5th edition – *DSM-5* (text revision).

American Psychiatric Association. (2003). *Practice guideline for the assessment and treatment of patients with suicidal behaviors*. https://psychiatryonline.org/pb/assets/raw/sitewide/practice_guidelines/guidelines/suicide.pdf

Andreasson, K., Krogh, J., Wenneberg, C., Jessen, H., Krakauer, K., Gluud, C., Thomsen, R., Randers, L., & Nordertoff, M. (2016). Effectiveness of dialectical behavior therapy versus collaborative assessment and management of suicidality treatment for reduction of self-harm in adults with borderline personality traits and disorder-a randomized observer-blinded clinical trial. *Depression and Anxiety, 33*(6), 520–530.

Anestis, M. D., Bryan, C. J., Capron, D. W., & Bryan, A. O. (2020). Lethal means counseling, distribution of cable locks, and safe firearm storage practices among the Mississippi National Guard: A factorial randomized controlled trial, 2018–2020. *American Journal of Public Health, 111*(2), 309–317. https://doi.org/10.2105/AJPH.2020.306019

Appleby, L., Kapur, N., Shaw, J., Hunt, I. M., Ibrahim, S., Turnbull, P., Bojanic, L., Rodway, C., Tham, S.-G., Richards, N., Burns, J., & NCISH staff. (2019). *The national confidential inquiry into suicide and safety in mental health. Annual report: England, Northern Ireland, Scotland and Wales*. University of Manchester. https://documents.manchester.ac.uk/display.aspx?DocID=46558

Appleby, L., Shaw, J., Amos, T., McDonnell, R., Harris, C., McCann, K., Kiernan, K., Davies, S., Bickley, H., & Parsons, R. (1999). Suicide within 12 months of contact with mental health services: National clinical survey. *British Medical Journal, 318*(7193), 1235–1239. https://doi.org/10.1136/bmj.318.7193.1235

Appleby, L., Shaw, J., Amos, T., McDonnell, R., Harris, C., & McCann, K. (2001). *Safety first: Five- year report of the national confidential inquiry into suicide and homicide by people with mental illness*. Department of Health Publications.

Asarnow, J. R., Berk, M., Hughes, J. L., & Anderson, N. L. (2015). The SAFETY program: A treatment-development trial of a cognitive-behavioral family treatment for adolescent suicide attempters. *Journal of clinical Child and Adolescent Psychology, 44*(1), 194–203. https://doi.org/10.1080/15374416.2014.940624

Asberg, M. (1997). Neurotransmitters and suicidal behavior: The evidence from cerebrospinal fluid studies. *Annals of the New York Academy of Sciences, 836*, 158–181. https://doi.org/10.1111/j.1749-6632.1997.tb52359.x

Aseltine, R. H., & DeMartino, R. (2004). An outcome evaluation of the SOS suicide prevention program. *American Journal of Public Health, 94*(3), 446–451. https://doi.org/10.2105/AJPH.94.3.446

Babalola, O., Gormez, V., Alwan, N. A., Johnstone, P., Sampson, S. (2014). Length of hospitalisation for people with severe mental illness. *Cochrane Database of Systematic Reviews, 2014*(1), CD000384. https://doi.org/10.1002/14651858.CD000384.pub3

Bagge, C., Connor, K., Reed, L., Dawkins, M., & Murray, K. (2015). Alcohol use to facilitate a suicide attempt: An event-based examination. *Journal of Studies on Alcohol and Drugs, 76*(3), 474–481. https://doi.org/10.15288/jsad.2015.76.474

Bagge, C., Littlefield, A., Connor, K., Sumaker, J., & Lee, H. (2014). Near-term predictors of the intensity of suicidal ideation: An examination of the 24 h prior to a recent suicide attempt. *Journal of Affective Disorders, 165*, 53–58. https://doi.org/10.1016/j.jad.2014.04.010

Baraff, L. J., Janowicz, N., & Asarnow, J. R. (2006). Survey of California emergency departments about practices for management of suicidal patients and resources available for their care. *Annals of Emergency Medicine, 48*(4), 452–458. https://doi.org/10.1016/j.annemergmed.2006.06.026

Barnes, L., Ikeda, R., & Kresnow, M. (2001). Help seeking behavior prior to nearly lethal suicide attempts. *Suicide and Life-Threatening Behavior, 32*(1 Suppl), 68–75.

Beautrais, A. L. (2004). Further suicidal behavior among medically serious suicide attempters. *Suicide and Life-Threatening Behavior, 34*(1), 1–11. https://doi.org/10.1521/suli.34.1.1.27772

Beautrais, A. L. (2007). The contribution to suicide prevention of restricting access to methods and sites. *Crisis, 28*(Suppl 1), 1–3. https://doi.org/10.1027/0227-5910.28.S1.1

Beck, A. T. (1996). Beyond belief: A theory of modes, personality, and psychopathology. In P. Salkovskis (Ed.), *Frontiers of cognitive therapy* (pp. 1–25). Guilford Press.

Beck, A. T., Brown, G., & Steer, R. (1989). Prediction of eventual suicide in psychiatric inpatients by clinical rating of hopelessness. *Journal of Consulting and Clinical Psychology, 57*(2), 309–310. https://doi.org/10.1037/0022-006X.57.2.309

Beck, A. T., Davis, J. H., Frederick, C. J., Perlin, S., Pokorny, A., Schulman, R. E., Seiden, R. H., & Wittlin, B. J. (1973). Classification and nomenclature. In H. Resnick & B. Hawthorne (Eds.), *Suicide prevention in the 70s* (pp. 7–12). US Government Printing Office.

Beck, A. T., Kovacs, M., & Weissman, A. (1979). Assessment of suicidal ideation: The scale for suicidal ideation. *Journal of Consulting and Clinical Psychology, 47*(2), 343–352. https://doi.org/10.1037/0022-006X.47.2.343

Beck, A. T., Steer, R. A., Kovacs, M., & Garrison, B. (1985). Hopelessness and eventual suicide: A 10-year prospective study of patients hospitalized with suicidal ideation. *American Journal of Psychiatry, 142*(5), 559–563. https://doi.org/10.1176/ajp.142.5.559

Bennett, B., Bricklin, P., Harris, E., Knapp, S., VandeCreek, L., & Younggren, J. (2006). *Assessing and managing risk in psychological practice: An individualized approach.* The Trust.

Berman, A., Jobes, D., & Silverman, M. (2006). *Adolescent suicide: Assessment and intervention* (2nd ed.). American Psychological Association.

Bohnert, A., & Ilgen, M. (2019). Understanding links among opioid use, overdose, and suicide. *New England Journal of Medicine, 380*(1), 71–79. https://doi.org/10.1056/NEJMra1802148

Bolton, I. (with Mitchell, C.) (1984). *My son, my son: A guide to healing after death, loss or suicide*. Bolton Press.

Bongar, B. (2002). *The suicidal patient: Clinical and legal standards of care*. American Psychological Association.

Bongar, B., Maris, R., Berman, A., & Litman, R. (1998). Outpatient standards of care and the suicidal patient. In B. Bongar, A. Berman, R. Maris, M. Silverman, E. Harris, & W. Packman (Eds.), *Risk management and suicidal patients* (pp. 4–33). Guilford Press.

Borges, G., Angst, J., Nock, M., Ruscio, A. M., Walters, E., & Kessler, R. (2006). A risk index for 12-month suicide attempts in the National Comorbidity Survey Replication (NCS-R). *Psychological Medicine, 36*(12), 1747–1757. https://doi.org/10.1017/S0033291706008786

Borges, G., Bagge, C., Cherpitel, C., Conner, K., Orozco, R., & Rossow, I. (2017). A meta-analysis of acute use of alcohol and the risk of suicide attempt. *Psychological Medicine, 47*(5), 949-957. https://doi.org/10.1017/S0033291716002841

Bostwick, J. M., & Pancratz, V. S. (2000). Affective disorders and suicide risk: A reexamination. *American Journal of Psychiatry, 157*(12), 1925–1932. https://doi.org/10.1176/appi.ajp.157.12.1925

Brent, D. (2001). Firearms and suicide. *Annals of the New York Academy of Sciences, 932*, 225–240. https://doi.org/10.1111/j.1749-6632.2001.tb05808.x

Brent, D., Baugher, M., Birmaher, B., Kolko, D., & Bridge, J. (2000). Compliance with recommendations to remove firearms in families participating in a clinical trial for adolescent depression. *Journal of the American Academy of Children and Adolescent Psychiatry, 39*(10), 1226–1228. https://doi.org/10.1097/00004583-200010000-00007

Brent, D., Perper, J., Moritz, G., Allman, C., Friend, A., Roth, C., Schweers, J., Balach, L., & Baugher, M. (1993a). Psychiatric risk factors for adolescent suicide: A case-control study. *Journal of the American Academy of Child and Adolescent Psychiatry, 32*(3), 521–529. https://doi.org/10.1097/00004583-199305000-00006

Brent, D., Perper, J., Moritz, G., Baugher, M., Roth, C., Balach, L., & Schweers, J. (1993b). Stressful life events, psychopathology and adolescent suicide: A case control study. *Suicide and Life-Threatening Behavior, 23*(3), 179–187.

Bridge, J. A., Asti, L., Horowitz, L. M., Greenhouse, J., Fontanella, C., Dheftall, A., Kelleher, K., & Campo, J. (2015). Suicide trends among elementary school–aged children in the United States from 1993 to 2012. *JAMA Pediatrics, 169*(7), 673–677. https://doi.org/10.1001/jamapediatrics.2015.0465

Brown, G., Jeglic, E., Henriques, G., & Beck, A. (2006). Cognitive therapy, cognition, and suicidal behavior. In T. Ellis (Ed.), *Cognition and suicide: Theory, research and therapy* (pp. 53–74). American Psychological Association.

Brown, G., Ten Have, T., Henriques, G., Nie, S., Hollander, J., & Beck, A. (2005). Cognitive therapy for the prevention of suicide attempts: A randomized controlled trial. *JAMA, 294*(5), 563–570. https://doi.org/10.1001/jama.294.5.563

Bruce, M. L., Ten Have, T. R., Reynolds, C. F. III, Katz, I., Schulberg, H. C., Mulsant, B. H., Brown, G. K., McAvay, G. J., Pearson, J. L., & Alexopulos, G. S. (2004). Reducing suicidal ideation and depressive symptoms in depressed older primary care patients: A randomized controlled trial. *Journal of the American Medical Association, 291*(9), 1081–1091. https://doi.org/10.1001/jama.291.9.1081

Bryan, C. J., Mintz, J., Clemans, T. A., Leeson, B., Burch, T. S., Williams, S. R., Maney, E., & Rudd, M. D. (2017). Effect of crisis response planning vs. contracts for safety on suicide risk in U.S. Army Soldiers: A randomized clinical trial. *Journal of Affective Disorders, 212*, 64–72.

Bryan, C. J., Rozek, D. C., Butner, J., & Rudd, M. D. (2019). Patterns of change in suicide ideation signal the recurrence of suicide attempts among high-risk psychiatric outpatients. *Behaviour Research and Therapy, 120*, 103392. https://doi.org/10.1016/j.brat.2019.04.001

Burstein, B., Agostino, H., & Greenfield, D. (2019). Suicidal attempts and ideation among children and adolescents in U.S. *emergency departments*, 2007–2015. *JAMA Pediatrics, 173*(6), 598–600.

Busch, K. A., Fawcett, J., & Jacobs, D. G. (2003). Clinical correlates of inpatient suicide. *Journal of Clinical Psychiatry, 64*(1), 14–19. https://doi.org/10.4088/JCP.v64n0105

Carroll, R., Metcalfe, C., & Gunnell, D. (2014). Hospital presenting self-harm and risk of fatal and non-fatal repetition: Systematic review and meta-analysis. *PlosOne*. https://doi.org/10.1371/journal.pone.0089944

Carter, G., Clover, K., Whyte, I., Dawson, A., & D'Este, C. (2005). Postcards from the Edge project: Randomised controlled trial of an intervention using postcards to reduce repetition of hospital treated deliberate self poisoning. *British Medical Journal, 331*(7520), 805. https://doi.org/10.1136/bmj.38579.455266.E0

Case, A., & Deaton, A. (2017). Mortality and morbidity in the 21st century. *Brookings Papers on Economic Activity, Spring*, 397–476. https://doi.org/10.1353/eca.2017.0005

Centers for Disease Control and Prevention (CDC). (2008). *Surveillance for violent deaths – national violent death reporting system*, 16 states, 2005. *Morbidity and Mortality Weekly Report, 57*(SS03), 1–43, 45.

Centers for Disease Control and Prevention (CDC). (2011). CDC health disparities and inequalities report – United States, 2011. *Morbidity and Mortality Weekly Report, 60*(Suppl). https://www.cdc.gov/mmwr/pdf/other/su6001.pdf

Centers for Disease Control and Prevention (CDC). (2020). *Trends in the prevalence of suicide-related behaviors. National YRBS: 1991–2019.* https://www.cdc.gov/healthyyouth/data/yrbs/factsheets/2019_suicide_trend_yrbs.htm

Centers for Disease Control and Prevention (CDC). (2021). Deaths: Final data for 2018. *National Vital Statistics Reports*, *69*(13), 1–83.

Chan, S. K., Chan, S. W., Pang, H. H., Yan, K. K., Hui, C. L. Chang, W. C., Lee, E. H., & Chen, E. Y (2018). Association of an early intervention service for psychosis with suicide rate among patients with first-episode schizophrenia-spectrum disorders. *JAMA Psychiatry, 75*(5), 458–464. https://doi.org/10.1001/jamapsychiatry.2018.0185

Cheng, A. T. A. (1995). Mental illness and suicide. *Archives of General Psychiatry*, *52*(7), 594–603. https://doi.org/10.1001/archpsyc.1995.03950190076011

Cherpitel, C., Borges, G., & Wilcox, H. (2004). Acute alcohol use and suicidal behavior: A review of the literature. *Alcoholism: Clinical and Experimental Research, 28*(5 Suppl), 18–28. https://doi.org/10.1097/01.ALC.0000127411.61634.14

Chessick, C. A., Perlick, D. A., Miklowitz, D. J., Kaczynski, R., Allen, M. H., Morris, C. D., & Marangel, L. B. (2007). Current suicidal ideation and past suicide attempts of bipolar patients as influences on caregiver burden. *Suicide and Life-Threatening Behavior, 37*, 482–491. https://doi.org/10.1521/suli.2007.37.4.482

Cipriani, A., Pretty, H., Hawton, K., & Geddes, J. (2005). Lithium in the prevention of suicidal behavior and all-cause mortality in patients with mood disorders: A systematic review of randomized trials. *American Journal of Psychiatry, 162*(10), 1805–1819. https://doi.org/10.1176/appi.ajp.162.10.1805

Clemons, J. T. (Ed.) (2001). *Children of Jonah: Personal stories by survivors of suicide.* Capital Books.

Comtois, K. A., Jobes, D. A., O'Connor, S., Atkins, D. C., Janis, K., Chessen, C., Landes, S. J., Holen, A., & Yuodelis Flores, C. (2011). Collaborative assessment and management of suicidality (CAMS): Feasibility trial for next-day appointment services. *Depression and Anxiety, 28*(11), 963–972. https://doi.org/10.1002/da.20895

Conner, K. R., & Bagge, C. L. (2019). Suicidal behavior: Links between alcohol use disorder and acute use of alcohol. *Alcohol Research: Current Reviews, 40*(1), 02. https://doi.org/10.35946/arcr.v40.1.02

Conner, K. R., Beautrais, A. L., & Conwell, Y. (2003). Risk factors for suicide and medically serious suicide attempts among alcoholics: Analyses of Canterbury suicide project data. *Journal of the Study of Alcoholism, 64*(4), 551–554. https://doi.org/10.15288/jsa.2003.64.551

Conner, K. R., & Duberstein, P. R. (2004). Predisposing and precipitating factors for suicide among alcoholics: Empirical review and conceptual integration. *Alcoholism: Clinical and Experimental Research, 28*(5 Suppl), 6S–17S.

Conner, K. R., Duberstein, P. R., & Conwell, Y. (1999). Age-related patterns of factors associated with completed suicide in men with alcohol dependence. *American Journal of Addictions, 8*(4), 312–318. https://doi.org/10.1080/105504999305712

Cooper, J., Kapur, N., Webb, R., Lawlor, M., Guthrue, E., Mackway-Jones, K., & Appleby, L. (2005). Suicide after deliberate self-harm: A 4-year cohort study. *American Journal of Psychiatry, 162*(2), 297-303. https://doi.org/10.1176/appi.ajp.162.2.297

Copeland, W., Goldston, D., Costello, E. (2017). Adult associations of childhood suicidal thoughts and behaviors: A prospective, longitudinal analysis. *Journal of the American Academy of Child and Adolescent Psychiatry, 56*(11), 958–965. https://doi.org/10.1016/j.jaac.2017.08.015

Currier, G., Fisher, S., & Caine, E. (2010). Mobile crisis team intervention to enhance linkage of discharged suicidal emergency department patients to outpatient psychiatric services: A randomized controlled trial. *Academic Emergency Medicine, 17*(1), 36–43. https://doi.org/10.1111/j.1553-2712.2009.00619.x

Cwik, M. F., Tingey, L., Maschino, A., Goklish, N., Larzelere-Hinton, F., Walkup, J., & Barlow, A. (2016). *Decreases in suicide deaths and attempts linked to the White Mountain Apache suicide surveillance and prevention system*, 2001–2012. *American Journal of Public Health, 106*(12), 2183–2189. https://doi.org/10.2105/AJPH.2016.303453

D'Augelli, A. R., Grossman, A. H., Salter, N. P., Starks, M. T., Vasey, J. J., & Sinclair, K. O. (2005). Predicting the suicide attempts of lesbian, gay, and bisexual youth. *Suicide and Life-Threatening Behavior, 35*(6), 646–660. https://doi.org/10.1521/suli.2005.35.6.646

Desîlets, A., Labossière, M., McGirr, A., & Turecki, G. (2016). Schizophrenia, other psychotic disorders, and suicidal behavior. In R. C. O'Connor, & J. Pirkis (Eds.), *The international handbook of suicide prevention* (pp. 93–109). John Wiley & Sons.

Diamond, G. S., Wintersteen, M. B., Brown, G. K., Diamond, G. M., Gallop, R., Shelef, K., & Levy, S. (2010). Attachment-based family therapy for adolescents with suicidal ideation: A randomized controlled trial. *Journal of the American Academy of Child & Adolescent Psychiatry, 49*(2), 122–131. https://doi.org/10.1037/e656972011-001

Didi Hirsch Mental Health Services Suicide Prevention Center. (2014). *Manual for support groups for suicide attempt survivors*. https://didihirsch.org/wp-content/uploads/Manual_for_Support_Groups_for_Suicide_Attempt_Survivors.pdf

The Dougy Center. (2001). *After a suicide: A workbook for grieving kids.* The Dougy Center.

Dube, S. R., Anda, R. F., Felitti, V. J., Chapman, D. P., Williamson, D. F., & Giles, W. H. (2001). Childhood abuse, household dysfunction, and the risk of attempted suicide throughout the life span: Findings from the Adverse Childhood Experiences Study. *Journal of the American Medical Association, 286*(24), 3126–3127. https://doi.org/10.1001/jama.286.24.3089

Dunne, E. (1992). Following a suicide: Postvention. In B. Bongar (Ed.), *Suicide: guidelines for assessment, management and treatment* (pp. 221–234). Oxford University Press.

Durkheim, E. (1951). *Suicide, a study in sociology* (J. A. Spaulding, & G. Simpson, Trans.). Routledge. (Original work published in 1897)

Dyches, B., Johnsen, G., & Oh, M. (2002). The impact of mobile crisis services on the use of community-based mental health services. *Research on Social Work Practice, 12*(6), 751–763. https://doi.org/10.1177/104973102237470

Eisenberg, M. E., & Resnick, M. D. (2006). Suicidality among gay, lesbian and bisexual youth: The role of protective factors. *Journal or Adolescent Health, 39*(5), 662–668. https://doi.org/10.1016/j.jadohealth.2006.04.024

Ellis, T., & Newman, C. F. (1996). *Choosing to live: How to defeat suicide through cognitive therapy*. New Harbinger.

Erlangsen, A., Lind, B. D., Stuart, E. A., Qin, P., Stenager, E., Larsen, K. J., Wang, A. G., Hvid, M., Nielsen, A. C., Pedersen, C. M., Winsløv, J.-H., Langhoff, C., Mühlmann, C., & Nordentoft, M. (2015). Short-term and long-term effects of psychosocial therapy provided to persons after deliberate self-harm: A register-based, nationwide multicentre study using propensity score matching. *Lancet Psychiatry*, *2*(1), 49–58.

Ertl, A., Sheats, K. J., Petrosky, E., Betz, C. J., Yuan, K., Fowler, K. A. (2019). Surveillance for violent deaths – National violent death reporting system, 32 States, 2016. *Surveillance Summaries, 68*(9), 1–36. https://doi.org/10.15585/mmwr.ss.6809a1

Farrow, T., Simpson, A., & Warren, H. (2002). The effects of the use of "no-suicide contracts" in community crisis situations: The experience of clinicians and consumers. *Brief Treatment and Crisis Intervention, 2*(3), 241–246. https://doi.org/10.1093/brief-treatment/2.3.241

Federal Communications Commission. (2020). *FCC designates 988 for the National Suicide Prevention Lifeline*. https://www.fcc.gov/document/fcc-designates-988-national-suicide-prevention-lifeline

Fergusson, D. M., Woodward, L. J., & Horwood, L. J. (2000). Risk factors and life processes associated with the onset of suicidal behavior during adolescence and early adulthood. *Psychological Medicine, 30*(1), 23–29. https://doi.org/10.1017/S003329179900135X

Fine, C. (1999). *No time to say goodbye.* Main Street Books.

Fleischmann, A., Betolote, J. M., Wasserman, D., De Leo, D., Bolhari, J., Botega, N. J. De Silva, D., Philips, M., Vijayakumar, L., Värnik, A., Schlebusch, L., Thanh, H. T. T. (2008). Effectiveness of brief intervention and contact for suicide attempters: A randomized controlled trial in five countries. *Bulletin of the World Health Organization, 86*, 703–709.

Fontanella, C. A., Warner, L. A., Steelesmith, D. L., Brock, G., Bridge, J. A., & Campo, J. V. (2020). Association of timely outpatient mental health services for youths after psychiatric hospitalization with risk of death by suicide. *JAMA Network Open*, *3*(8), e2012887. https://doi.org/10.1001/jamanetworkopen.2020.12887

Friedman, R. (2014). Antidepressants' black-box warning – ten years later. *New England Journal of Medicine, 371*(18), 1666–1668. https://doi.org/10.1056/NEJMp1408480

Garraza, G. L., Kuiper, N., Goldston, D., McKeon, R., & Walrath, C. (2019). Long-term impact of the Garrett Lee Smith Youth Suicide Prevention Program on youth suicide mortality, 2006–2015. *Journal of Child Psychology and Psychiatry, 60*(10), 1142–1147. https://doi.org/10.1111/jcpp.13058

Geller, J. L., Fisher, W. H., & McDermeit, M. (1995). A national survey of mobile crisis services and their evaluation. *Psychiatric Services, 46*(9), 893–897. https://doi.org/10.1176/ps.46.9.893

Gibb, S., Beautrais, A., & Fergusson, D. (2005). Mortality and further suicidal behavior after an index suicide attempt: A 10-year study. *Australia and New Zealand Journal of Psychiatry, 39*(1–2), 95–100. https://doi.org/10.1080/j.1440-1614.2005.01514.x

Gibbons, R. D., Brown, C. H., Hur, K., Marcus, S. M., Bhaumik, D. K., Erkens, J. A., Herings, R. M., & Mann, J. J. (2007a). Early evidence on the effects of regulators' suicidality warnings on SSRI prescriptions and suicide in children and adolescents. *American Journal of Psychiatry, 164*(9), 1356–1363. https://doi.org/10.1176/appi.ajp.2007.07030454

Gibbons, R. D., Brown, C. H., Hur, K., Marcus, S. M., Bhaumik, D. K., & Mann, J. J. (2007b). Relationship between antidepressants and suicide attempts: An analysis of the Veterans Health Administration data sets. *American Journal of Psychiatry, 164*(7), 1044–1049. https://doi.org/10.1176/ajp.2007.164.7.1044

Goldman-Mellor, S., Olfson, M., Lidon-Moyano, C., & Schoenbaum, M. (2019). *Association of suicide and other mortality with emergency department presentation, JAMA Psychiatry, 2*(12), e1917571. https://doi.org/10.1001/jamanetworkopen.2019.17571

Goldman-Mellor, S., Olfson, M., Lidon-Moyano, C., & Schoenbaum, M. (2020). Mortality following nonfatal opioid and sedative/hypnotic drug overdose. *American Journal of Preventive Medicine, 59*(1), 59–67. https://doi.org/10.1016/j.amepre.2020.02.012

Goldney, R. D. (1998). Variations in suicide rates: The tipping point. *Crisis, 19*(3), 136–138. https://doi.org/10.1027/0227-5910.19.3.136

Gould, M., Lake, A., Galfalvy, H., Kleinman, M., Munfakh, J., Wright, J., & McKeon, R. (2017). Follow-up with callers to the National Suicide Prevention Lifeline: Evaluation of callers' perceptions of care. *Suicide and Life-Threatening Behavior*, *48*(1), 75–86.

Gould, M. S., Kalafat, J., Harris Munfakh, J. L., & Kleinman, M. (2007). An evaluation of hotline outcomes, part 2: Suicide callers. *Suicide and Life-Threatening Behavior, 37*(3), 338–352. https://doi.org/10.1521/suli.2007.37.3.338

Griffith, G. (2005). *Will's choice*. Harper Collins.

Gruenbaum, M. F., Galfaly, H. C., & Choo, T. H. (2018). Ketamine for rapid reduction of suicidal thoughts in major depression: A midazolam-controlled randomized clinical trial. *American Journal of Psychiatry, 175*(4), 327–335. https://doi.org/10.1176/appi.ajp.2017.17060647

Gutheil, T. G. (1990). Argument for the defendant-expert opinion: Death in hindsight. In R. I. Simon (Ed.), *Review of clinical psychiatry and the law* (pp. 335–339). American Psychiatric Association.

Gysin-Maillart, A., Schwab, S., Soravia, L., Megert, M., & Michel, K. A. (2016). Novel brief therapy for patients who attempt suicide: A 24-months follow-up randomized controlled study of the attempted suicide short intervention program (ASSIP). *PLoS medicine, 13*(3), e1001968. https://doi.org/10.1371/journal.pmed.1001968

Hawton, K. (2005). *Prevention and treatment of suicidal behavior.* Oxford University Press.

Hendin, H., Haas, A., Maltsberger, J., Koestner, B., & Szanto, K. (2006). Problems in psychotherapy of suicidal patients. *American Journal of Psychiatry, 163*(1), 67–72. https://doi.org/10.1176/appi.ajp.163.1.67

Horowitz, L. M., Bridge, J. A., Teach, S. T., Ballard, E., Klima, J., Rosenstein, D. L., Wharff, E. A., Ginnis, K., Cannon, E., Joshi, P., & Pao, M. (2012). Ask suicide screening question: A brief instrument for the pediatric emergency department. *Archives of Pediatric Adolescent Medicine, 166*(12), 1170–1176. https://doi.org/10.1001/archpediatrics.2012.1276

Hugo, M., Smout, M., & Bannister, J. (2002). A comparison in hospitalization rates between a community-based mobile emergency service and a hospital-based emergency service. *Australian and New Zealand Journal of Psychiatry, 36*(4), 504–508. https://doi.org/10.1046/j.1440-1614.2002.01042.x

Ilgen, M. A., Bohnert, A. S., Ganoczy, D., Bair, M. J., McCarthy, J. F., & Blow, F. C. (2016). Opioid dose and risk of suicide. *Pain, 157*(5), 1079–1084. https://doi.org/10.1097/j.pain.0000000000000484

Inskip, H., Harris, E., & Barraclough, B. (1998). Lifetime risk of suicide for affective disorder, alcoholism, and schizophrenia. *British Journal of Psychiatry, 172*, 35–37. https://doi.org/10.1192/bjp.172.1.35

Isometsa, E., & Lonnqvist, J. K. (1998). Suicide attempts preceding completed suicides. *British Journal of Psychiatry, 173*(6), 531-535. https://doi.org/10.1192/bjp.173.6.531

Institute of Medicine. (2007). *Hospital-based emergency care: At the breaking point*. The National Academies Press. https://doi.org/10.17226/11621

Institute of Medicine, Goldsmith, S., Pellmar, T., Kleinman, A., & Bunney, W. (2002). *Reducing suicide: A national imperative.* National Academies Press. https://doi.org/10.17226/10398

Jamison, K. R. (1999). *Night falls fast.* Random House.

Jobes, D. (2006). *Managing suicidal risk: A collaborative approach.* Guilford Press.

Jobes, D. A., Comtois, K. A., Gutierrez, P., Brenner, L., Huh, D., Chalker, S., Ruhe, G., Kerbrat, A., Atkins, D., Jennings, K., Crumlish, J., Coron, C., O' Connor, S., Hendricks, E., Schembari, B., Singer, B. & Crow, B. (2017). A randomized controlled trial of the collaborative assessment and management of suicidality versus enhanced care as usual with suicidal soldiers. *Psychiatry, 80*(4), 339–356.

Jobes, D., Eyman, J., & Yufit, R. (1995). How clinicians assess suicide risk in adolescents and adults. *Crisis Intervention & Time-Limited Treatment, 2*(1), 1–12.

Joiner, T. (2005). *Why people die by suicide.* Harvard University Press.

Joiner, T., Kalafat, J., Draper, J., Stokes, H., Knudson, K., Berman, A., & McKeon, R. (2007). Establishing standards for the assessment of suicide risk among callers to the national suicide prevention lifeline. *Suicide and Life-Threatening Behavior, 37*(3), 353–365. https://doi.org/10.1521/suli.2007.37.3.353

Joiner, T., Simpson, S., Rogers, M., Staney, I., & Galynker, I. (2018). *Whether called acute suicidal affective disturbance or suicide crisis syndrome, a suicide-specific diagnosis would enhance clinical care, increase patient safety, and mitigate clinician liability, Journal of Psychiatric Practice, 24*(4), 274–278. https://doi.org/10.1097/PRA.0000000000000315

The Joint Commission. (2007). *National patient safety goals*. https://www.jointcommission.org/standards/national-patient-safety-goals/

The Joint Commission. (2008). *Sentinel event statistics – June 30, 2008*. https://www.jointcommission.org/resources/patient-safety-topics/sentinel-event/sentinel-event-data-summary/

Kann, L., McManus, T., Harris, W. A., Shanklin, S. L., Flint, K. H., Queen, B., Lowry, R., Chyen, D., Whittle, L., Thornton, J., Lim, C., Bradford, D., Yamakawa, Y., Leon, M., Brener, N., & Ethier, K. A. (2018). *Surveillance Summaries, 67*(8), 1–114. https://doi.org/10.15585/mmwr.ss6708a1

Kapur, N., & Goldney, R. (2019). *Suicide prevention* (3rd ed.). Oxford University Press.

Karch, D. L., Barker, L., & Strine, T. W. (2006). Race/ethnicity, substance abuse and mental illness among suicide victims in 13 states: 2004 data from the National Violent Death Reporting System. *Injury Prevention*, *12*(Suppl. II), 22–27. https://doi.org/10.1136/ip.2006.013557

Kaslow, N. J., Thompson, M. P., Okun, A., Price, A., Young, S., Bender, M., Wyckoff, S., Twomey, H., Goldin, J., & Parker, R. (2002). Risk factors for suicide attempts among African American women. *Journal of Consulting and Clinical Psychology, 70*(2), 311–319. https://doi.org/10.1037/0022-006X.70.2.311

Katz, I., Peltzman, T., Jedele, J., & McCarthy, J. (2019). Critical periods for increased mortality after discharge from inpatient mental health units: Opportunities for prevention. *Psychiatric Services, 70*(6), 450–456. https://doi.org/10.1176/appi.ps.201800352

Kessler, R. C., Warner, C. H., Ivany, C., Petukhova, M. V., Rose, S., Bromet, E. J., Brown, M., Cai, T., Colpe, L. J., Cox, K. L., Fullerton, C. S., Gilman, S. E., Gruber, M. J., Heeringa, S. G., Lewandowski-Romps, L., Li, J., Millikan-Bell, A. M., Naifeh, J. A., Knock, M. K., Rosselini, A. J., … Army STARRS Collaborators. (2015). Predicting suicides after psychiatric hospitalization in US Army soldiers: The Army study to assess risk and resilience in servicemembers (Army STARRS). *JAMA Psychiatry, 72*(1), 49–57.

King, C. A., Arango, A., Kramer, A., Busby, D., Czyz, E., Foster, C. E., Gillespie, B. W., & YST Study Team. (2019). Association of the youth-nominated support team intervention for suicidal adolescents with 11- to 14-year mortality outcomes: Secondary analysis of a randomized clinical trial. *JAMA Psychiatry, 76*(5), 492–498. https://doi.org/10.1001/jamapsychiatry.2018.4358

King, C. A., Brent, D., Grupp-Phelan, J., Casper, C., Dean, J. M., Chernick, L. S., Fein, J. A., Mahabee-Gittens, M., Patel, S. J., Mistry, R. D., Duffy, S., Melzer-Lange, M., Rogers, A., Cohen, D. M., Keller, A., Shenoi, R., Hickey, R. W., Rea, M., ... Gibbons, R. (2021). Prospective development and validation of the Computerized Adaptive Screen for Suicidal Youth. *JAMA Psychiatry, 78*(5), 540–549. https://doi.org/10.1001/jamapsychiatry.2020.4576

Kleespies, P. M., Penk, W. E., & Forsyth, J. P. (1993). The stress of patient suicidal behavior during clinical training: Incidence, impact and recovery. *Professional Psychology: Research and Practice, 24*(3), 293–303. https://doi.org/10.1037/0735-7028.24.3.293

Klonsky, E.D., & May, A. M. (2015). The three-step theory (3ST): A new theory of suicide rooted in the ideation to action framework. *International Journal of Cognitive Therapy, 8*(2), 114–129. https://doi.org/10.1521/ijct.2015.8.2.114

Klonsky, E. D., May, A. M., & Glenn, C. R. (2013). *The relationship between non-suicidal self-injury and attempted suicide: Converging evidence from four samples, Journal of Abnormal Psychology, 122*(1), 231–237. https://doi.org/10.1037/a0030278

Knox, K. L., Litts, D. A., Talcott, G. W., Feig, J. C., & Caine, E. D. (2003). Risk of suicide and related adverse outcomes after exposure to a suicide prevention program in the US Air Force: Cohort study. *British Medical Journal, 327*, 1376–1381. https://doi.org/10.1136/bmj.327.7428.1376

Koons, C. R., Robins, C. J., Tweed, J. L., Lynch, T. R., Gonzalez, A. M., Morse, J. Q., Bishop, G. K., Butterfield, M. I., & Bastian, L. A. (2001). Efficacy of dialectical behavior therapy in women veterans with borderline personality disorder. *Behavior Therapy, 32*(2), 371–390. https://doi.org/10.1016/S0005-7894(01)80009-5

Kruesi, M. J. P., Grossman, J., Pennington, J. M., Woodward, P. J., Duda, D., & Hirsch, J. G. (1999). Suicide and violence prevention: Parent education in emergency department. *Journal of the American Academy of Child and Adolescent Psychiatry, 38*(3), 250–255. https://doi.org/10.1097/00004583-199903000-00010

Large, M., Kaneson, M., Myles, N., Myles, H., Gunaratne, P., & Ryan, C. (2016). Meta-analysis of longitudinal cohort studies of suicide risk assessment among psychiatric patients: Heterogeneity of results and lack of improvement over time. *PLoS ONE, 11*(6), e0156322. https://doi.org/10.1371/journal.pone.0156322

Lewis, L. M. (2007). No suicide contracts: A review of what we know. *Suicide and Life-Threatening Behavior, 37*(1), 50–57. https://doi.org/10.1521/suli.2007.37.1.50

Lewitzka, U., Sauer, C., Bauer, M., & Felber, W. (2019). Are national suicide prevention programs effective? A comparison of four verum and four control counties over 30 years. *BMC Psychiatry, 19,* 158. https://doi.org/10.1186/s12888-019-2147-y

Lezine, D. (with Brent, D.) (2008). *Eight stories up: An adolescent chooses hope over suicide.* Oxford University Press.

Linehan, M. M. (1981). *Suicidal Behaviors Questionnaire* [Unpublished manuscript]. University of Washington.

Linehan, M. M. (1993). *Cognitive behavioral treatment of borderline personality disorder.* Guilford Press.

Linehan, M. M. (2008). Suicide intervention research: A field in desperate need of development. *Suicide and Life-Threatening Behavior, 38*(5), 483–485. https://doi.org/10.1521/suli.2008.38.5.483

Linehan, M. M., Comtois, K., Murray, A., Brown, M., Gallup, R., Heard, H., Korslund, K. E., Tutek, D. A., Reynolds, S. K., & Lindenboim, N. (2006). Two-year randomized control trial and follow up of dialectical behavior therapy vs. therapy by experts for suicidal behaviors and borderline personality disorder. *Archives of General Psychiatry, 63*(7), 757–766.

Linehan, M. M., Goodstein, J., Nielsen, S., & Chiles, J. (1983). Reasons for staying alive when you are thinking of killing yourself: The Reasons for Living Inventory. *Journal of Consulting and Clinical Psychology, 51*(2), 276–286. https://doi.org/10.1037/0022-006X.51.2.276

Linehan, M. M., Schmidt, H., Dimeff, L. A., Kanter, J. W., Craft, J. C., Kanter, J., & Comtois, K. A. (1999). Dialectical behavior therapy for patients with borderline personality disorder and drug-dependence. *American Journal on Addiction, 8*(4), 279–292. https://doi.org/10.1080/105504999305686

Linn-Gust, M. (2001). *Do they have bad days in heaven*? Bolton Press.

Luoma, J. B., Martin, C. E., & Pearson, J. L. (2002). Contact with mental health and primary care providers before suicide: A review of the evidence. *American Journal of Psychiatry, 159*(6), 909–916. https://doi.org/10.1176/appi.ajp.159.6.909

Mann, J. J., & Currier D. M., (2010) Stress, genetics, and epigenetics effects on the neurobiology of suicidal behavior and depression. *European Psychiatry, 25*(5), 268–271.

Maris, R. W. (1981). *Pathways to suicide: A survey of self-destructive behavior*. Oxford University Press.

Maris, R. W. (1992). The relationship of nonfatal suicide attempts to completed suicides. In R.W. Maris, A. Berman, J. Maltsberger, & R. Yufit (Eds.), *Assessment and prediction of suicide* (pp. 362–380). Guilford Press.

Maris, R. W. (2007). A comment on Robert D. Goldney's "A historical note on suicide during the course of treatment for depression." *Suicide and Life-Threatening Behavior, 37*(1), 600–601.

May, P., Serna, P., Hurt, L., & DeBruyn, L. (2005). Outcome evaluation of a public health approach to suicide prevention in an American Indian tribal nation. *American Journal of Public Health, 95*(7), 1238–1244. https://doi.org/10.2105/AJPH.2004.040410

McCauley, E., Berk, M.S., Asarnow, J. R., Adrian, M., Cohen, J., Korslund, K., Avina, C., Hughes, J., Harned, M., Gallop, R., & Linehan, M. M. (2018). Efficacy of dialectical behavior therapy for adolescents at high risk for suicide: A randomized clinical trial. *JAMA Psychiatry, 75*(8), 777–785. https://doi.org/10.1001/jamapsychiatry.2018.1109

McNiel, D. E., Gregory, A. L., Lam, J. N., Binder, R. L., & Sullivan, G. R. (2003). Utility of decision support tools for assessing acute risk of violence. *Journal of Consulting and Clinical Psychology, 71*(5), 945–953. https://doi.org/10.1037/0022-006X.71.5.945

Mehlum, L., Tørmoen, A. J., Ramberg, M., Haga, E., Diep, L. M., Laberg, S., Larsson, B. S., Stanley, B. H., Miller, A. L., Sund, A. M., & Grøholt, B. (2014). Dialectical behavior therapy for adolescents with repeated suicidal and self-harming behavior: A randomized trial. *Journal of the American Academy of Child and Adolescent Psychiatry, 53*(10), 1082–1091. https://doi.org/10.1016/j.jaac.2014.07.003

Melle, I., & Barrett E. (2012). Insight and suicidal behavior in first-episode schizophrenia. *Expert Review of Neurotherapeutics, 12*(3), 353-359. https://doi.org/10.1586/ern.11.191

Meltzer, H. Y. (1999). Suicide and schizophrenia: Clozapine and the InterSePT study. International Clozaril/Leponex Suicide Prevention Trial. *Journal of Clinical Psychiatry, 60*(Suppl. 12), 47–50.

Meyers, M., & Fine, C. (2006). *Touched by suicide: Hope and healing after suicide*. Gotham Books.

Miller, A. L., Rathus, J. H., & Linehan, M. M. (2007). *Dialectical behavior therapy with suicidal adolescents*. Guilford.

Miller, I., Camargo, C., Arias, S., Sullivan, A., Allen, M., Goldstein, A., Manton, A. P., Espinola, J. A., Jones, R., Hasegawa, K., Boudreaux, E., & ED-SAFE Investigators.

(2017). Suicide prevention in an emergency department population: The ED-SAFE Study. *JAMA Psychiatry, 74*(6), 563–570. https://doi.org/10.1001/jamapsychiatry.2017.0678
Millner, A. J., Lee, M. D., & Nock, M. K. (2017). Describing and measuring the pathway to suicide attempts: A preliminary study. *Suicide and Life-Threatening Behavior, 47*(3), 353–369. https://doi.org/10.1111/sltb.12284
Minnesota Office of Ombudsman for Mental Health and Developmental Disabilities. (2002). *Suicide prevention alert.* https://mn.gov/omhdd/assets/suicide-prevention-alert_tcm23-27671.pdf
Molnar, B. E., Buka, S. I., & Kessler, R. C. (2001). Child sexual abuse and subsequent psychopathology: Results from the National Comorbidity Study. *American Journal of Public Health, 91*(5), 753–760. https://doi.org/10.2105/AJPH.91.5.753
Moscicki, E. K. (2001). Epidemiology of completed and attempted suicide: Toward a framework for prevention. *Clinical Neuroscience Research, 1*(5), 310–323. https://doi.org/10.1016/S1566-2772(01)00032-9
Moskos, M. A., Olson, L. M., Halbern, S., Keller, T., & Gray, D. (2005). Utah youth suicide study: Psychological autopsy study. *Suicide and Life-Threatening Behavior, 35*(5), 536–546. https://doi.org/10.1521/suli.2005.35.5.536
Motto, J. (1976). Suicide prevention for high risk patients who refuse treatment. *Suicide and Life-Threatening Behavior, 6*(4), 223–230.
Motto, J., & Bostrum, A. (2001). A randomized control trial of post crisis suicide prevention. *Psychiatric Services, 52*(6), 828–833. https://doi.org/10.1176/appi.ps.52.6.828
Murphy, G. E., & Robbins, E. (1967). Social factors in suicide. *Journal of the American Medical Association, 199*(5), 81–86.
Murphy, G. E., Armstrong, J. W., Hermele, S. I., Fischer, J. R., & Clendenin, W. W. (1979). Suicide and alcoholism: Interpersonal loss confirmed as a predictor. *Archives of General Psychiatry, 36*(1), 65–69. https://doi.org/10.1001/archpsyc.1979.01780010071007
Murray, D. (2016). Is it time to abandon suicide risk assessment? *BJPsych Open, 2*(1), e1–e2M. https://doi.org/10.1192/bjpo.bp.115.002071
National Action Alliance for Suicide Prevention. (2016). *Crisis now: Transforming services is within our reach.* https://theactionalliance.org/sites/default/files/crisisnow.pdf
National Action Alliance for Suicide Prevention: Transforming Health Systems Initiative Work Group. (2018). *Recommended standard care for people with suicide risk: Making health care suicide safe*. Education Development Center, Inc.
Niederkrotenthaler, T., Logan, J., Karch, D., & Crosby, A. (2014). Characteristics of US suicide decedents in 2005–2010 who had received mental health treatment. *Psychiatric Services, 65*(3), 387–390. https://doi.org/10.1176/appi.ps.201300124
Nock, M., Borgas, G., Bromet, E., Alonso, J., Angermeyer, M., Beautrais, A., et al. (2008). Cross-national prevalence and risk factors for suicidal ideation, plans and attempts. *British Journal of Psychiatry, 192*(2), 98–105. https://doi.org/10.1192/bjp.bp.107.040113
Nordentoft, M., Mortensen, P., & Pedersen, C. (2011). Absolute risk of suicide after first hospital contact in mental disorder. *Archives of General Psychiatry, 68*(10), 1058–1064. https://doi.org/10.1001/archgenpsychiatry.2011.113
O'Connor, R. (2011). *The integrated motivational-volitional model of suicidal behavior, Crisis, 32*(6), 295–298. https://doi.org/10.1027/0227-5910/a000120
Orbach, I. (1997). A taxonomy of factors related to suicidal behavior. *Clinical Psychology: Science and Practice, 4*(3), 208–224. https://doi.org/10.1111/j.1468-2850.1997.tb00110.x
Owens, J., Fingar, P., Heslin, K., Mutter, K., & Booth, C. (2017). Emergency department visits related to suicidal ideation, 2006–2013. *AHRQ Statistical Brief # 220.* https://www.hcup-us.ahrq.gov/reports/statbriefs/sb220-Suicidal-Ideation-ED-Visits.jsp
Owens, D., Horrocks, J., & House, A. (2002). Fatal and non-fatal repetition of self-harm: Systematic review. *The British Journal of Psychiatry, 181*, 193–199. https://doi.org/10.1192/bjp.181.3.193
Pappas, S. (2021). New research in suicide prevention: With suicide rates stubbornly high, researchers are digging into the details of who is most at risk – and when. *Monitor on Psychology, 52*(6). https://www.apa.org/monitor/2021/09/news-suicide-prevention

Paris, J. (2019). Suicidality in borderline personality disorder. *Medicina, 55*(6), 223. https://doi.org/10.3390/medicina55060223

Pirkola, S. P., Isometsa, E. T., Heikkenin, M. E., Henriksson, M. M., Marttunen, M. J., & Lönnqvist, J. K. (1999). Female psychoactive substance-dependent suicide victims differ from male – results from a nationwide psychological autopsy study. *Comprehensive Psychiatry, 40*(2), 101–107. https://doi.org/10.1016/S0010-440X(99)90113-X

Piscopo, K., Lipari, R. N., Cooney, J., & Glasheen, C. (2016). *Suicidal thoughts and behavior among adults: Results from the 2015 National Survey on Drug Use and Health.* https://www.samhsa.gov/data/sites/default/files/NSDUH-DR-FFR3-2015/NSDUH-DR-FFR3-2015.htm

Posner, K., Oquendo, M., Gould, M., Stanley, B., & Davies, M. (2007). Columbia classification algorithm of suicide assessment (C-CASA): Classification of suicidal events in the FDA's pediatric suicidal risk analysis of anti-depressants. *American Journal of Psychiatry, 164*(7), 1035–1043. https://doi.org/10.1176/ajp.2007.164.7.1035

Powell, V., Barber, C., Hedegaard, H., Hempstead, K., Hull-Jilly, D., Shen, X., Thorpe, G. E., & Weis, M. A. (2006). Using NVDRS data for suicide prevention: promising practices in seven states. *Injury Prevention*, 12(Suppl. *II)*, 28–32. https://doi.org/10.1136/ip.2006.012443

Preuss, U. W., Schuckit, M. A., Smith, T. L., Danko, G. P., Buckman, K., Bierut, L., Bucholz, K. K., Hesselbrock, M. N., Hesselbrock, V. M., & Reich, T. (2002). Comparison of 3190 alcohol-dependent individuals with and without suicide attempts. *Alcoholism: Clinical & Experimental Research, 26*(4), 471–477. https://doi.org/10.1111/j.1530-0277.2002.tb02563.x

Range, L. M., & Knott, E. C. (1997). Twenty suicide assessment instruments: Evaluation and recommendations. *Death Studies, 21*(1), 25–58. https://doi.org/10.1080/074811897202128

Range, L. M., Leach, M., McIntyre, D., Posey-Deters, P., Marion, M., Kovac, S., Baños, J. H., & Vigil. J. (1999). Multicultural perspectives on suicide. *Aggression and Violent Behavior, 4*(4), 413—430. https://doi.org/10.1016/S1359-1789(98)00022-6

Rihmer, Z., Rihmer, A., & Dome, P. (2015). Suicidal behaviour in patients with mood disorders. *Evidence Based Psychiatric Care, 1*, 19–26.

Rogers, J., & Oney, K. (2005). Clinical use of suicide assessment scales: Enhancing reliability and validity through the therapeutic relationship. In R. Yufit & D. Lester (Eds.), *Assessment, treatment and prevention of suicidal behavior* (pp. 7–27). John Wiley & Sons.

Rotheram-Borus, M. J., Piacentini, J., Cantwell, C., Belin, T. R., & Song, J. (2000). The 18-month impact of an emergency room intervention for adolescent female suicide attempters. *Journal of Consulting and Clinical Psychology, 68*(6), 1081–1093. https://doi.org/10.1037/0022-006X.68.6.1081

Roy, A., Rylander, G., & Sarchiapone, M. (1997). Genetics of suicide: Family studies and molecular genetics. *Annals of the New York Academy of Sciences, 836*, 135–157. https://doi.org/10.1111/j.1749-6632.1997.tb52358.x

Rudd, M. D., Bryan, C. J., Wertenberger, E. G., Peterson, A. L., Young-McCaughan, S., Mintz, J., Williams, S. R., Arne, K. A., Breitbach, J., Delano, K., Wilkinson, E, & Bruce, T. O. (2015). Brief cognitive-behavioral therapy effects on post-treatment suicide attempts in a military sample: Results of a randomized clinical trial with 2-year follow-up. *American Journal of Psychiatry, 172*(5), 441–449.

Rudd, M. D., Joiner, T., & Rahab, M. H. (2001). *Treating suicidal behavior: An effective time limited approach.* Guilford Press.

Safer, D. J., & Zito, J. M. (2007). Do antidepressants reduce suicide rates? *Journal of the Royal Institute of Public Health, 121*(4), 274–277. https://doi.org/10.1016/j.puhe.2006.09.024

Sanford, C., Marshall, S. W., Martin, S. I., Coyne-Beasley, T., Walker, A. E., Cook, P. J., Norwood, T., & Demissie, Z. (2006). Deaths from violence in North Carolina: How deaths differ in females and males. *Injury Prevention*, 12(Supp. *II)*, 10–16.

Schaffer, A. Sinyor, M., Kurdyak, P., Vigod, S., Sareen, J., Reis, C., Green, D., Bolton, J. Rhodes, A., Grigoriasis, S., Cairney, J., & Cheung, A. (2016). *Population based analy-*

sis of health are contacts among suicide decedents: Identifying opportunities for more targeted suicide prevention strategies, World Psychiatry, 15(2), 135–145.

Shuck, A., Calati, R., Barzilay, S., Elkouby, S. & Galynker, I. (2019). *Suicide crisis syndrome: A review of supporting evidence for a new suicide-specific diagnosis, Behavioral Sciences & the Law, 39*(3), 1–17. https://doi.org/10.1002/bsl.2397

Schuckit, M. A., Tipp, J. E., Bergman, M., Reich, W., Hesselbrock, V. M., & Smith, T. L. (1997). Comparison of induced and independent major depressive disorders in 2,945 alcoholics. *American Journal of Psychiatry, 154*(7), 948–957. https://doi.org/10.1176/ajp.154.7.948

Scott, R. L. (2000). Evaluation of a mobile crisis program: Effectiveness, efficiency and consumer satisfaction. *Psychiatric Services, 51*(9), 1153–1156. https://doi.org/10.1176/appi.ps.51.9.1153

Shea, S. (2002). *The practical art of suicide assessment: A guide for mental health professionals and substance abuse counselors.* John Wiley & Sons.

Shneidman, E. S. (1996). *The suicidal mind.* Oxford University Press.

Shneidman, E. S. (2004). *Autopsy of a suicidal mind.* Oxford University Press.

Shulsinger, R., Kety, S., Rosenthal, D., & Wender, P. (1979). A family study of suicide. In M. Schou & E. Stromgren (Eds.), *Origins, prevention and treatment of affective disorders* (pp. 277–287). Academic Press.

Silverman, M. M., Berman, A. L., Sanddal, N. D., O'Carroll, P. W., & Joiner, T. E. (2007a). Rebuilding the Tower of Babel: A revised nomenclature for the study of suicide and suicide related behaviors. Part 1: Background, rationale, and methodology. *Suicide and Life-Threatening Behavior, 37*(3), 248–263. https://doi.org/10.1521/suli.2007.37.3.248

Silverman, M. M., Berman, A. L., Sanddal, N. D., O'Carroll, P. W., & Joiner, T. E. (2007b). Rebuilding the Tower of Babel: A revised nomenclature for the study of suicide and suicide related behaviors. Part 2: Suicide-related ideations, communications, and behaviors. *Suicide and Life-Threatening Behavior, 37*(3), 264–277. https://doi.org/10.1521/suli.2007.37.3.264

Simon, R. (1999). The suicide prevention contract: clinical, legal and risk management issues. *Journal of the American Academy of Psychiatry and the Law, 27*(3), 445–450.

Simon, R. (2004). *Assessing and managing suicide risk: Guidelines for clinically based risk management.* American Psychiatric Association.

Simon, R. (2006). Imminent suicide: The illusion of short-term prediction. *Suicide and Life-Threatening Behavior, 36*(3), 296–301. https://doi.org/10.1521/suli.2006.36.3.296

Simon, R. (2007). Gun safety management with patients at risk for suicide. *Suicide and Life-Threatening Behavior, 37*(5), 518–525. https://doi.org/10.1521/suli.2007.37.5.518

Simon, G. E., Coleman, K. J., Rossom, R. C., Beck, A., Oliver, M., Johnson, E., Whiteside, U., Operskalski, B., Penfold, R. B., Shortreed, S. M., & Rutter, C. (2016). Risk of suicide attempt and suicide death following completion of the Patient Health Questionnaire depression module in community practice. *The Journal of Clinical Psychiatry*, *77*(2), 221–227. https://doi.org/10.4088/JCP.15m09776

Simon, T., Swann, A., Powell, K., Potter, L., Kresnow, M., & O'Carroll, P. (2001). Characteristics of impulsive suicide attempts and attempters. *Suicide and Life-Threatening Behavior, 32*(1 Suppl), 49–59.

Skog, O. (1991). Alcohol and suicide: Durkheim revisited. *Acta Sociologica, 34*(3), 193–206. https://doi.org/10.1177/000169939103400303

Slee, N., Garnefski, N., van der Leeden, R., Arensman, E., & Spinhoven, P. (2008). Cognitive-behavioural intervention for self-harm: Randomised controlled trial. *British Journal of Psychiatry, 192*(3), 202–211. https://doi.org/10.1192/bjp.bp.107.037564

Stanley, B., & Brown, G. (2012). Safety planning intervention: A brief intervention to mitigate suicide risk. *Cognitive and Behavioral Practice, 19*(2), 256–264. https://doi.org/10.1016/j.cbpra.2011.01.001

Stanley, B., Brown, G., Brenner, L., Galfalvey, H., Currier, G., Knox, K., Chaudhury, S., Bush, A., & Green, K. (2018). Comparison of the safety planning intervention with follow up vs usual care of suicidal patients treated in the emergency department. *JAMA Psychiatry, 75*(9), 894–900. https://doi.org/10.1001/jamapsychiatry.2018.1776

Stanley, B., Martínez-Alés, G., Gratch, I., Rizk, M., Galfalvy, H., Choo, T.-H., & Mann, J. J. (2021). Coping strategies that reduce suicidal ideation: An ecological momentary assessment study. *Journal of Psychiatric Research, 133*, 32–37. https://doi.org/10.1016/j.jpsychires.2020.12.012

Stanley, M., & Stanley, B. (1989). Biochemical studies in suicide victims: Current findings and future implications. *Suicide and Life-Threatening Behavior, 19*(1), 30–42. https://doi.org/10.1111/j.1943-278X.1989.tb00364.x

Stone, D. M., Simon, T. R., Fowler, K. A., Kegler, S. R., Yuan, K., Holland, K. M., Ivey-Stephenson, A. Z., & Crosby, A. E. (2018). Vital signs: Trends in state suicide rates – United States, 1999–2016 and circumstances contributing to suicide – 27 states, 2015. *Morbidity and Mortality Weekly Review, 67*(22), 617-624. https://www.cdc.gov/mmwr/volumes/67/wr/mm6722a1.htm https://doi.org/10.15585/mmwr.mm6722a1

Styron, W. (1990). *Darkness visible*. Vintage Books.

Substance Abuse and Mental Health Services Administration. (2003). *National Survey on Drug Use and Health: Risk of suicide among Hispanic females aged 12–17.*

Substance Abuse and Mental Health Services Administration. (2006). *Suicidal thoughts, suicide attempts, major depressive episode, and substance abuse among adults.*

Substance Abuse and Mental Health Services Administration. (2018). *Key substance abuse and mental health indicators in the United States: Results from the 2017 National Survey on Drug Use and Health* (HHS Publication No. SMA 18-5068, NSDUH series H-53). https://www.samhsa.gov/data/sites/default/files/cbhsq-reports/NSDUHFFR2017/NSDUHFFR2017.htm

Substance Abuse and Mental Health Services Administration. (2020). *National guidelines for behavioral health crisis care: Best practice toolkit.* https://www.samhsa.gov/sites/default/files/national-guidelines-for-behavioral-health-crisis-care-02242020.pdf

Substance Abuse and Mental Health Services Administration. (2021). *Key substance use and mental health indicators in the United States: Results from the 2020 National Survey on Drug Use and Health* (HHS Publication No. PEP21-07-01-003, NSDUH Series H-56). https://www.samhsa.gov/data

Sudol, K., & Oquendo M. A. (2016). Visualizing the suicidal brain: Neuroimaging and suicide prevention. In R. C. O'Connor & J. Pirkis (Eds.), *International handbook of suicide prevention* (pp. 188–205). Wiley Blackwell.

Taipale, H., Lähteenvuo, M., Tanskanen, A., Mittendorfer-Rutz, E., & Tiihonen, J. (2020). Comparative effectiveness of antipsychotics for risk of attempted or completed suicide among persons with schizophrenia. *Schizophrenia Bulletin*, sbaa111. https://doi.org/10.1093/schbul/sbaa111

Teasdale, J. D., Segal, Z. V., Williams, J. M. G., Ridgeway, V., Soulsby, J., & Lau, M. (2000). Prevention of relapse/recurrence in major depression by mindfulness-based cognitive therapy. *Journal of Consulting and Clinical Psychology, 68*(4), 615–623. https://doi.org/10.1037/0022-006X.68.4.615

US Department of Defense. (2015). *Department of Defense Strategy for Suicide Prevention.*

US Department of Health and Human Services. (2012). *National Strategy for Suicide Prevention: Goals and objectives for action. A report of the U.S. Surgeon General and of the National Action Alliance for Suicide Prevention.* https://theactionalliance.org/resource/revised-national-strategy-suicide-prevention-2012

US Department of Health and Human Services. (2001). *National Strategy for Suicide Prevention: Goals and objectives for action* (DHHS Publication No. SMA-3517). https://www.ncbi.nlm.nih.gov/books/NBK44281/

US Department of Veterans Affairs. (2018). *National Strategy for Preventing Veteran Suicide 2018–2028.*

US Food & Drug Administration. (2018). *Suicidality in children and adolescents being treated with antidepressant medications.* https://www.fda.gov/drugs/postmarket-drug-safety-information-patients-and-providers/suicidality-children-and-adolescents-being-treated-antidepressant-medications

Valenstein, M., Hyungjin, M., Ganoczy, D., McCarthy, J., Ziven, K., Austin, K., Hogett, K., Eisenberg, D., Piette, J., Blow, F., & Olfson, M. (2009). Higher-risk periods for suicide among VA patients receiving depression treatment: Prioritizing suicide prevention efforts. *Journal of Affective Disorders, 112*(1–3), 50–58. https://doi.org/10.1016/j.jad.2008.08.020

van der Sande, R., van Rooijen, E., Buskens, E., Allart, E., Hawton, K., van der Graaf, Y., van Engeland, H. (1997). Intensive in-patient and community intervention versus routine care after attempted suicide. A randomised controlled intervention study. *British Journal of Psychiatry, 171*, 35–41. https://doi.org/10.1192/bjp.171.1.35

Vajani, M., Annest, J., Crosby, A., Alexander, J., & Millet, L. (2007). Nonfatal and fatal self-harm injuries among children aged 10–14 years: United States and Oregon, 2001–2003. *Suicide and Life-Threatening Behavior, 37*(5), 493–506. https://doi.org/10.1521/suli.2007.37.5.493

Walsh, B. W. (2006). *Treating self-injury*. Guilford.

Waterhouse, J., & Platt, S. (1990). General hospital admission in the management of parasuicide. A randomised controlled trial. *British Journal of Psychiatry, 156*, 236–42. https://doi.org/10.1192/bjp.156.2.236

Weis, M. A., Bradberry, C., Carter, L. P., Ferguson, J., & Kozareva, D. (2006). An exploration of human services system contacts prior to suicide in South Carolina: An expansion of the South Carolina National Violent Death Reporting System, *Injury Prevention, 12*(Suppl. II), 17–21. https://doi.org/10.1136/ip.2006.012427

Welu, T. C. (1977). A follow-up program for suicide attempters: Evaluation of effectiveness. *Suicide and Life-Threatening Behavior, 7*(1), 17–20.

Witkiewitz, K., Roos, C. R., Colgan, D. D., & Bowen, S. (2017). *Mindfulness*. Hogrefe Publishing. https://doi.org/10.1027/00414-000

Williams, J. M., Barnhofer, T., Crane, C., & Dugan, D. (2006). The role of overgeneral memory in suicidality. In T. Ellis (Ed.), *Cognition and suicide: Theory, research and practice* (pp. 173–192). American Psychological Association.

Wise, T. (2012). *Waking up*. Pathfinder Publications.

While, D., Bickley, H., Roscoe, A., Windfuhr, K., Rahman, S., Shaw, J., Appleby, L., & Kapur, N. (2012). *Implementation of mental health service recommendations in England and Wales and suicide rates*, 1997–2006: A cross-sectional and before-and-after observational study. *Lancet, 379*(9820), 1005–1012. https://doi.org/10.1016/S0140-6736(11)61712-1

Woolf, S., & Schoomaker, H. (2019). *Life expectancy and mortality rates in the United States*, 1959–2017. *JAMA, 322*(10), 1996–2016. https://doi.org/10.1001/jama.2019.16932

World Federation for Mental Health. (2006). *Building awareness – reducing risk: Mental illness and suicide*. http://wmhd2021.com/index.php

World Health Organization. (2014). *Preventing suicide: A global imperative*. https://apps.who.int/iris/handle/10665/131056

World Health Organization. (2018). *National suicide prevention strategies: Progress examples and indicators*. https://www.who.int/mental_health/suicide-prevention/national_strategies_2019/en/

World Health Organization. (2019a). *International classification of diseases, 10th revision, clinical modification (ICD-10-CM)*. https://www.cdc.gov/nchs/icd/icd10cm.htm

World Health Organization. (2019b). *Suicide in the world: Global health estimates*. https://apps.who.int/iris/handle/10665/326948

World Health Organization. (2021). *Suicide worldwide in 2019: Global health estimates*. https://www.who.int/publications/i/item/9789240026643

Appendix: Tools and Resources

The materials reproduced on the following pages can also be downloaded free of charge from the Hogrefe website after registration.

Appendix 1: Outline for Suicide Consultation
Appendix 2: Decision Tree for Intervening With Suicidal Callers

How to proceed:

1. Create a user account (or, if you have already one, please log in)

For customers from the USA, Canada, and the rest of the world:
hgf.io/login-us

For European customers:
hgf.io/login-eu

2. Download your supplementary materials

Go to **My supplementary materials** in your account dashboard and enter the code below. You will automatically be redirected to the download area, where you can access and download the supplementary materials.

Code: B-CI19XO

To make sure you have permanent direct access to all the materials, we recommend that you download them and save them on your computer.

Outline for Suicide Consultation

I. Reason for Referral

II. History of Suicidal Thoughts, Feelings, and Behaviors

1. Precipitant for most recent episode of suicidality

a) Family or other interpersonal precipitants
b) Psychological/emotional precipitants
c) Health precipitants
d) Other precipitants, i.e., social, financial, etc.

2. Psychological state during most recent episode of suicidality

a) Mental status variables
Degree of disorientation vs. ability to accurately test reality, (including psychosis, intoxication, etc.), insight, judgment, mood, affect, degree of perturbation, presence of psychiatric symptoms
b) Suicide risk variables
Suicidal ideation including: frequency, intensity, intrusiveness, sense of felt control over ideation, degree of suicidal intent, thinking about methods, availability of method, degree of suicidal planning, preparatory behaviors, degree to which plans had been initiated into action, suicidal threats and communications, whether attempt made and rating of lethality, behaviors intended to aid rescue vs. behaviors intended to conceal discovery

3. Protective factors

Degree to which suicidal ideas or impulses have been able to be resisted, ability to tolerate distress, deal with ambivalence, tolerate frustration, future orientation, attitude toward help seeking, interpersonal connectedness, ability to sustain connectedness and hope in face of loss, impulse control, strength of therapeutic alliance

4. Vulnerabilities

Loss of sustaining resource, psychiatric illness, modeling of suicide within the family and degree of identification, cognitive vulnerabilities, impulsivity

5. Past suicide history

(List for each past suicidal attempt or episode of acute suicidality)

a) Precipitants: family/interpersonal, cognitive, emotional/psychological, biological, social/financial
b) Suicidal state and behaviors: intent, degree of planning, rating of lethality, rescue-ability, degree of impulsivity, degree of perturbation, reaction to attempt

6. Consequences of suicidal behavior

Functional analysis, interpersonal effects, relief vs regret

This page may be reproduced by the purchaser for clinical use.
From: R.T. McKeon: *Suicidal behavior* (2nd ed.)
© 2022 Hogrefe Publishing

III. Risk Assessment

Summary of factors contributing to elevated risk: family/interpersonal, cognitive, emotional/psychological, biological, social, financial, psychiatric illness, suicide history

Projected risk for suicide:

1. Imminent
2. Short-term
3. Long-term

Recommended intervention strategies to decrease suicidal risk: (include whenever possible treatment or intervention strategies specifically targeted to decreasing previously identified suicide risk factors).

Interventions should be considered to alter both precipitants and vulnerabilities.

This page may be reproduced by the purchaser for clinical use.
From: R.T. McKeon: *Suicidal behavior* (2nd ed.) © 2022 Hogrefe Publishing

Decision Tree for Intervening With Suicidal Callers

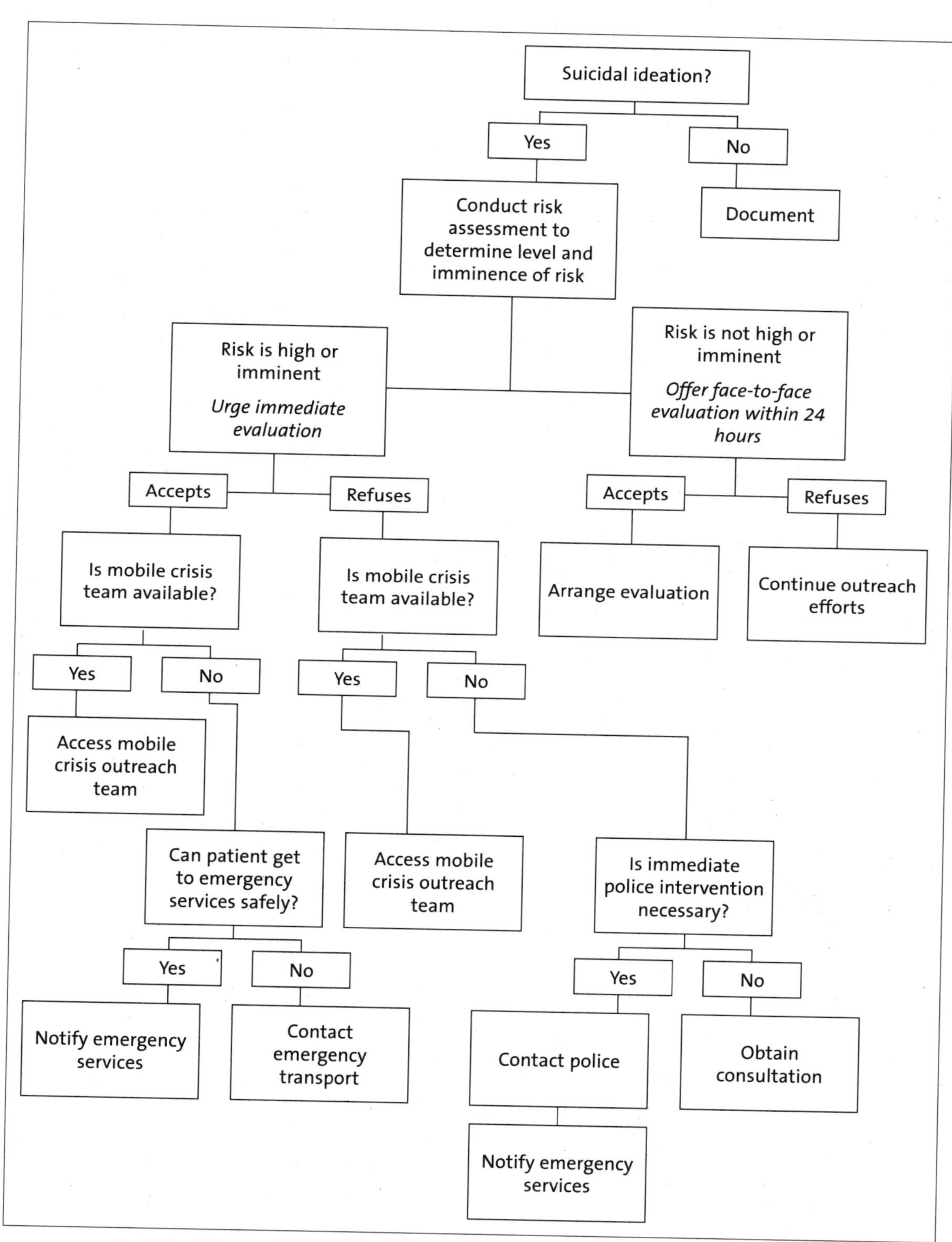

This page may be reproduced by the purchaser for clinical use.
From: R.T. McKeon: *Suicidal behavior* (2nd ed.)
© 2022 Hogrefe Publishing